Pearls of Wisdom
For Everyday Living

For Your Personal and
Professional Growth

Pearls of Wisdom For Everyday Living

For Your Personal and Professional Growth

Rev. Amos L. Lewis

The Master of Simplicity

An Amethyst Moon book

AMETHYST MOON
PUBLISHING

Pearls of Wisdom for Everyday Living

Unless otherwise indicated, all Scripture quotations are taken from the King James Version of the Bible.

An Amethyst Moon Book
Published by AMETHYST MOON PUBLISHING
P.O. Box 87885
Tucson, AZ 85754
www.onechoicecanchangealife.com

ISBN 978-0-9792426-5-6 (13 digit)
0-9792426-5-7 (10 digit)

∞∞∞

Proverbs 3:13-16 says, "Blessed is the man who finds wisdom, the man who gains understanding, 14 for she is more profitable than silver and yields better returns than gold. 15 She is more precious than rubies; nothing you desire can compare with her. 16 Long life is in her right hand; in her left hand are riches and honor." (New International Version)

∞∞∞

A proverb is a short sentence based on long experience.
(Miguel De Cervantes)

∞∞∞

God's Word is God's Wisdom for your Life (Deut. 4:5-6).

God sent His Son but He left His Book. (Mike Murdock)

∞∞∞

Methods are many, principles are few, methods change, but principles never do. (Rick Warren)

Principles are universal and unchanging laws that help us understand how the world works so we can successfully navigate our way safely through the challenges of life. (Rev. Amos L. Lewis)

CONTENTS

WHY I WROTE THIS BOOK

I wrote this book because I have a passion to help people reach their full potential and fulfill their God-given destiny. I want you to excel and do well in every area of your life. To reach your maximum potential you will need both a coach and a cheerleader. Please consider me to be both. Therefore, I have written this book to help you safely navigate your way through the challenges of life.

HOW TO USE THIS BOOK

This is a unique book. It is not a book to be read and filed away or put on your bookshelf. It is a book to be devoured and digested. Read it during your quiet time and meditate on these pearls and passages. Take this book with you to work, school or wherever you go. Highlight those pearls that speak to you. Write in your own notes and discoveries as well. As you learn and apply these principles, your life will be transformed. After your transformation, go out and share these pearls with others. In fact, I believe this book would make a great gift for your family, friends, and co-workers. The Bible says that wisdom is better than wealth (Prov. 3:13-16). It's one of life's greatest gifts. Now you have in your hands the ability to give the gift of wisdom.

◇◇

Give me a hundred men who fear nothing but sin, and desire nothing but God, and I will shake the world. I care not a straw whether they be clergymen or laymen; and such alone will overthrow the kingdom of Satan and build up the Kingdom of God on earth. (John Wesley)

◇◇

SCOPE OF THIS WORK

Like Solomon I have read widely and wisely (for the last 30 years) gathering these jewels (1 Kings 4:29-34; Eccl. 12:9-10). I have read from Confucius to Christ, from the Bible to the best business books on the market, from philosophy to psychology. I have taken what I've read and learned and filtered it through the Word (Rom. 3:4a). What you hold in your hand is your *"Scriptural Success System."* Real success is first spiritual then physical, mental then material, and internal then external (3 John 2).

PROOF IN THE PUDDING

The information in this book is not about hype. It contains timeless principles that will help you. These principles have helped me build a successful marriage, family, military career, church and business. This book doesn't deal with theories but truth, and if applied, these principles will transform your life. These principles will work if you work them. Don't worry about people or circumstances in which you have no control. Just focus on working the principles and watch them work for you. God is not a respecter of persons, but He is a respecter of principles.

∞∞

What lies behind us and what lies before us are small matters compared to what lies within us. (Ralph Waldo Emerson)

The heights by great men reached and kept were not attained by sudden flight, but they, while their companions slept, were toiling upward in the night. (Henry Wadsworth Longfellow)

∞∞

For the Lord gives wisdom, and from his mouth comes knowledge and understanding. (Proverbs 2:6, NIV)

DEDICATION

I want to dedicate this book to my wife, Zeannie Lewis. She has been my companion for almost 25 years. I appreciate her patience, understanding and support. Quite often I slip out of the bed to pray, read or write. She understands my calling and passion better than anyone else on the planet. My ministry would not be the success it is today without her loving support. She is my soul mate for life.

I dedicate this book to my children: Kelvin, Jenelle, Terria, and Jeremiah. They have willingly shared their father with the church and community unselfishly for over 21 years. I dedicate this book to my grandsons as well: Jayden L. Lewis and Emmanuel Z. Holmes. I pray that they will grow up to be champions for Christ.

I dedicate this book to my parents (Sarah Lewis and the late John T. Lewis) who instill a love for God in me at an early age. They didn't send me to church; they took me to church! I really appreciate my godly heritage. It was after the death of my father (who was the chairman of the deacon board for over 50 years at Greater St. Paul Missionary Baptist Church in Pinckard, Alabama) that the Lord spoke to me and said, "Pursue wisdom." My father never spent a day in his life in school. He had to work all his life. In a way, this was to my advantage in the sense that God gave him wisdom where he lacked a formal education (James 1:5). He was able to lead a church and community for over 50 years because of his wisdom. I also dedicate this book to my sisters Doris Howard and Vivian Lewis-Thompson and my brother Joe Lewis.

I dedicate this book also to all those who help raised me; the members of Greater St. Paul Missionary Baptist Church and the people of Pinckard, Alabama where I grew up. They all had a hand in raising me, and for that I'm truly grateful.

Lastly, but not least, I dedicate this book to the Rising Star Missionary Baptist Church family. They took a chance on this young preacher at the age of 27. I didn't know anything about pastoring and very little about life. Nevertheless, by the grace of God, we have had a 21-year love affair. I plan to spend the next 19 years of my life leading and feeding these precious people of God. They have watched me grow. They have helped me grow into the man, pastor and leader I am today. May God richly bless them for their love and support!

The Lord spoke to my heart a while back and told me that it is time for me to launch my writing career. This book is my first attempt at putting something of real value in writing. I hope it proves to be a blessing to your life as you gain wisdom for the journey ahead.

> **This book contains a wealth of wisdom for everyday living.
> You hold in your hands the keys to the treasures of life.**

ACKNOWLEDGEMENTS

I want to acknowledge the A. L. Lewis Ministries team (Michelle Nobles, David Baxter, Terry Thomas, and Joe Jackson) for their unselfish dedication. They work very hard volunteering their time and effort to make the ministry work. I also want to acknowledge the staff members at Rising Star; Linda Milton, Mandy Castain, and Cynthia Carr-Person. They help keep the day-to-day operations of the church going so I can do all the things I do.

Finally, I want to pay special recognition to Tandala Kidd who serves in so many capacities. I want to thank her for all she does. She is involved in every aspect of my ministry: A. L. Lewis Ministries, Rising Star, Southern Arizona Missionary Baptist District Association, and the Interdenominational Ministerial Alliance. She unselfishly gives of herself. A person of her talent and commitment is very rare. She does everything without any need of recognition or fanfare. Truly, she has a servant's heart.

INTRODUCTION

In the following pages you will find over 1,000 quotes and wise sayings that I have collected or created over the last 21 years. I've always had a love for catchy sayings and rhymes.

After being approached by several people in the church and the community, I decided to go back over the last 21 years of preaching and 48 years of living and put them in writing.

It is my sincere desire that these pearls of wisdom will help you as much as they have helped me. I believe the short and concise lines of truth will be easy for you to remember and apply.

I would encourage you to read these quotes during your devotional time or leisure. Let them spark your imagination and then you can come up with some of your own sayings or quotes. We are all the product of the things we have seen, heard or read. Nobody is an original at everything. In life we learn from one another.

I think these sayings or quotes will help our high-tech generation of young people to grab these truths and retain them and most of all apply them to everyday life. I've noticed down through the years that nobody really likes sermons. People very seldom remember a "great" sermon. However, I do know that people remember catchy sayings, quotes, illustrations and stories.

Anyway, this is my attempt to put my quotes and sayings in writing for my family, friends and the public at large. I hope they will prove to be a blessing to you like they have been to me.

— *Rev. Amos L. Lewis*

THE PEARLS OF WISDOM

1. Life is governed by laws and principles. Obey them and excel. Disobey them and you'll fail (Exodus 20:3-17).

☆

2. One great line of wisdom can be enough to change your entire life (Prov. 4:7).

☆

3. The only difference between an acorn and an oak tree is time (Eccl. 3:11; Luke 2:39-40).

☆

4. What happens in your mind will eventually happen in time (Job 3:25).

☆

5. You can't lead people where you don't go. And you can't teach what you don't know (1 Tim. 4:11-12; Hos. 4:9).

☆

6. Success is meeting needs, healing hurts, and solving problems for others with excellence and gratitude (Luke 10:30-37).

☆

7. You have been blessed to be a blessing (Gen. 12:2). Become a channel of God's blessings to others (Luke 12:48).

☆

8. The church should be a blessing to the community not a burden on the community (Matt. 25:34-40).

☆

9. Failure isn't fatal unless you flake out before you finish (2 Tim. 4:6-8).

☆

10. Mistakes are the tuition we pay for our education on the way to success (Prov. 24:16).

☆

11. Self-help is the best form of help. Don't expect others to do for you what you can do for yourself (John 5:1-9).

☆

12. Ten two-letter words that will empower you: "If it is to be, it is up to me" (Gal. 6:4-5). This is called "responsibility."

☆

13. Real Christianity is both vertical and horizontal. It reaches up to God and out to mankind (Luke 10:27).

☆

14. You won't stumble, fumble or crumble if you learn to stay humble (1 Cor. 10:12; Dan. 4:37; Prov. 8:13).

☆

15. Faith is acting like God told the truth (Num. 23:19).

☆

16. Obedience is the real proof of faith (James 2:17; 1 Sam. 15:22).

☆

17. Your priorities in life should be God, family, church and then the community and ultimately the world (1 Tim. 3:4-5).

☆

18. Speak life rather than death. There is power in your words so watch what you say (Prov. 18:21).

☆

19. If God is your partner, make big plans (Rom. 8:31; Jer. 29:11).

☆

20. Obedience to the will of God is the pathway to real prosperity (Josh. 1:8; Ps. 1:1-3; Is. 1:19).

☆

21. Service to others will increase your self-worth and net-worth. Therefore, the way up is down (Mark 10:35-45).

☆

22. Life is meant for movement. When you stop you drop (1 Sam. 4:17; Acts 17:28).

☆

23. It is better to endure the pain of change than the regret of staying the same (Luke 19:41-44).

☆

24. Readers are leaders and leaders are readers (Josh. 8:35; 1 Tim. 4:17).

☆

25. What you read affects what you believe (Rom. 10:17).

☆

26. When you mess up, admit it and quit it (Prov. 28:13).

☆

27. His presence creates passion and power for life (Ps. 16:11).

☆

28. People who are unteachable are unreachable (Acts 8:9-24).

☆

29. He who thinks he knows everything is a fool (Prov. 12:15).

☆

30. Disconnect from destructive people (Ps. 1:1). This is called "blessed subtraction" (Rom. 16:17-18).

☆

31. Your talent creates your treasure and your gifts create your gold in life (Prov. 18:16).

☆

32. Invest in yourself because you are your greatest asset. (Benjamin Franklin)

☆

33. People act funny about their money (Acts 5:1-11).

☆

34. Those who sin with you will eventually sin against you because wicked people do not live by a moral code (Judges 16:1-31).

☆

35. Happiness in life is based upon your relationships with people and your completion of God-given projects (John 17:1-4).

☆

36. Work isn't a dirty four letter word, but a gift from God (Gen. 2:8; Eccl. 5:18-20).

☆

37. The quality of your questions will determine the quality of your answers (Matt. 16:13-16).

☆

38. Giving purifies your heart and lightens your load (Matt. 6:19-21; 1 Tim. 6:17-19).

☆

39. Whatever you do in life make it neat, sweet and hard to beat. (Rev. J. R. Cunningham)

☆

40. Never refuse a life jacket if you are drowning (Matt. 14:22-33).

☆

41. Never subtract from your character or calling to add to your popularity (1 Kings 22:1-18).

☆

42. It is never the size of the problem; but it's always the size of the person (Acts 27:21-25).

☆

43. Little people have big problems and big people have little problems (Matt. 8:23-27).

☆

44. In life you can organize or agonize. "Create a SYSTEM so you can Save YourSelf Time, Energy and Money". (Robert Allen)

☆

45. Listen to your quiet inner voice. It's your conscience telling you which way to go (Prov. 3:5-6; Rom. 8:14).

☆

46. Do only what you are good at and let others do what you can't do well (Gal. 2:8). Stay in your strength zone.

☆

47. Follow your heart and make your life a work of art (Eccl. 9:10).

☆

48. Do what you love and love what you do because what you love loves you (Eccl. 9:10).

☆

49. The proof of passion is pursuit. We only pursue what we really love and value (Hosea 3:1-5).

☆

50. Those who are good at making excuses are seldom good at anything else. (Benjamin Franklin)

☆

51. The wise work for a living while the fool depends upon luck (2 Thes. 3:10-12).

☆

52. It is better to work and get paid nothing than to get paid and do nothing (Prov.s 10:4; 12:24; 13:4; 21:5).

☆

53. Plan your work and work your plan (Exodus 26:30).

☆

54. Preparation and perspiration will get you to your destination (Gen. 3:19; 1 Thes. 5:12; Rom. 16:12).

☆

55. After you get through dreaming, wake up and get busy making your dream come true (Prov. 6:10-11).

☆

56. The good thing about the future is that it comes one day at a time. (Abraham Lincoln)

☆

57. Tomorrow is the coming attraction, but today is the main event. Enjoy today and make the best of it (Matt. 6:34; Ps. 118:24).

☆

58. Yesterday is dead; tomorrow is yet unborn. Your life is today (Ps. 118:24).

☆

59. Your words are creating your world. In the long run you will have what you say if you believe it and act on it (Mark 11:24).

☆

60. The first person you lead is you (1 Cor. 11:1). If you won't follow yourself, why should anybody else?

☆

61. Your passion is a clue to your purpose and calling in life (Jer. 1:5; 20:9). Your calling should be your career.

☆

62. What you believe determines what you receive (Matt. 9:29).

☆

63. Don't let your self-worth be determined by your net-worth (Luke 12:15).

☆

64. Your team must be equal to your dream. You can't win the Kentucky Derby with mules or donkeys (Matt. 17:1-13).

☆

65. No one is indispensable. If you don't believe me, I dare you to die (Isaiah 6:1).

☆

66. The content person knows when he has had enough (1 Tim. 6:6). It's not about what you have but what you are.

☆

67. When speaking in public: Stand up to be seen, speak up to be heard, and sit down to be appreciated. (Nido Qubein)

☆

68. Self-control will keep you from losing control (1 Cor. 9:27).

☆

69. If you want to be healed, you must learn to forgive (Matt. 6:14). Not forgiving others can literally make you sick.

☆

70. Dress for success (Gen. 41:14)! People will judge you based upon what they see (1 Sam. 16:7). Only God can see your heart.

☆

71. You can't improve on nature. Learn to appreciate God's beautiful creation (Gen. 1:31; Ps. 19:1).

☆

72. Respect for God is the first step in gaining wisdom (Prov. 1:7).

☆

73. Create a pleasant environment by surrounding yourself with good music, sweat fragrances and live plants (1 Sam. 16:14-16).

☆

74. The quality of your decisions determines the quality of your life (Duet. 30:15-16).

☆

75. You will see the hand of God when you stop trusting the hand of man (Jer. 17:5).

☆

76. You can't fix what you tolerate. If you make yourself a door mat, people will walk all over you (Gal. 2:11-14; James 4:7).

☆

77. I will study and get ready, then maybe my chance will come. (Abraham Lincoln)

☆

78. You need proper rest to be at your best (Ps. 127:2).

☆

79. Don't expect tomorrow's provision today (Matt. 6:11).

☆

80. All of your labor will never be able to compete with God's favor (Dan. 1:9).

☆

81. To be average means being on top of the bottom. Never be proud of being average. (Bishop Paul S. Morton)

☆

82. Your vision is a potential picture of your future (Hab. 2:2-3).

☆

83. To keep growing you have to keep going. Expose yourself to great places and people on a regular basis (Acts 2:5).

☆

84. Suffering strengthens the soul. Too much comfort and ease make the soul soft and weak (1 Pet. 5:10).

☆

85. Only send out in words, thoughts or deeds the things in life you want to receive (Gal. 6:7).

☆

86. The good that you do will come back to you (Gal. 6:9).

☆

87. The best control in the world is self-control (Prov. 16:32).

☆

88. If you can master yourself, you can master life (1 Cor. 9:27).

☆

89. No one can achieve real greatness without self-discipline (1 Cor. 9:24-27; 2 Tim. 2:21).

☆

90. Pay your bills first and live on the rest (2 Kings 4:1-7).

☆

91. Average people are motivated by pain or pleasure. Great people are motivated by purpose (Acts 20:24; 2 Tim. 4:6-8).

☆

92. Dig your well before you get thirsty. (Chinese Proverb)

☆

93. There is nothing permanent except change. (Herodotus)

☆

94. Those who drink the water must not forget those who dug the well. (Africa Proverb)

☆

95. The size of the battle determines the size of the reward (1 Sam. 17:1-51).

☆

96. Circumstances do not make a man; they reveal him. (John Hubbard)

☆

97. Character is what a man is in the dark. (D. L. Moody)

☆

98. If you aren't debt free, then you're not totally free (Prov. 22:7).

☆

99. Too many people want the Wealth of Solomon but not the Wisdom of Solomon (2 Chron. 1:7-12).

☆

100. The seasons in life are fixed. Keep being faithful and giving and eventually your season will come (Gen. 8:22; Gal. 6:9).

☆

101. It takes team work for the dream to work (Eccl. 4:9-12).

☆

102. Provision is only promised at the place of your assignment. Where God guides He provides (Gen. 22:14 & 1 Kings 17:1-16).

☆

103. If you do not teach your children the ways of the Lord, the Devil will teach them the ways of sin. (Charles H. Spurgeon)

☆

104. Find your niche and stay in your lane or else you'll get run over (Gal. 1:15-17).

☆

105. Distraction is a deadly weapon. Don't allow people to break your focus (Phil. 3:13). Broken focus leads to failure.

☆

106. Time and knowledge will enlarge you and your world (Luke 2:40, 52).

☆

107. Character is determined by choice, not by chance. (Aristotle)

☆

108. No success can compensate for failure in the home. (David O. McKay)

☆

109. Create a dream wall or dream book of what you want to be, do or have. If you can see it, you can be it (Neh. 6:15-16).

☆

110. Build a team to help you with your dream. No one succeeds alone in life (Eccl. 4:9-12).

☆

111. To think long term, invest in people. Pass on what you know to others (2 Tim. 2:2). Think generational (Exodus 3:15-17)!

☆

112. You need cheerleaders and coaches to help you reach your full potential (Heb. 12:1-2).

☆

113. Thoughts have presence. You can sense what a person is thinking or feeling (Matt. 12:25).

☆

114. Birds of a feather do flock together (Prov. 13:20).

☆

115. Uncommon vision requires uncommon provision. God will provide you with both if you make Him your focus (Ps. 84:11).

☆

116. Thankfulness leads to increase while ingratitude leads to loss (Luke 15:11-31).

☆

117. You are not a loser if you learn from your mistakes (Luke 22:32).

☆

118. Fight for feedback and if it's valid, follow it (Prov. 12:15).

☆

119. Never be afraid of the truth because the truth is your friend (John 8:32).

☆

120. Make everything very clear and simple. Small people hide behind big words (Mark 13:37).

☆

121. Go where the fish are biting. Sell your products and services to those who value what you have to offer (John 1:10-13).

☆

122. A big dream will require a big team. If you can accomplish your dream alone, then your dream is too small (Matt. 12:1-4).

☆

123. Know your limitations. You are not Superman or Wonder Woman (Ps. 103:13-16).

☆

124. Structure determines growth. You can't build a skyscraper on a chicken coop foundation (Ps. 127:1; Matt. 7:24-27).

☆

125. Staff your weaknesses. No one is good at everything (Rom. 12:6-8). Others are there to complete you not to compete with you.

☆

126. Good customer service is essential in any organization. If you aren't friendly, people don't care what you're selling (1 Kings 5:1).

☆

127. Manage with your head but lead with your heart (2 Chron. 10:6-15). You must love people before you can lead them.

☆

128. Remove bad apples prayerfully and quickly. Low morale is bad for business (Prov. 26:20-28).

☆

129. Conduct allowed is conduct approved and repeated (1 Sam. 3:11-14).

☆

130. There isn't much difference between the devil and a rebel (Isaiah 14:12-15).

☆

131. Wisdom is sanctified common sense (1 Chron. 22:12-13).

☆

132. Common sense isn't that common (Job 28:20-21, 28).

☆

133. Information is the key to transformation (Rom. 12:2).

☆

134. Train, trade or terminate unproductive people (1 Tim. 1:18-20).

☆

135. Mentor your children by the lessons you give and by the life you live. Some things are better caught than taught (Eph. 6:1-4).

☆

136. The best gift you can give to your child is you (Eph. 6:1-4).

☆

137. Give a grateful person more than what she asks for (Luke 17:12-19).

☆

138. Use technology to organize and simplify every area of your life (1 Cor. 14:40).

☆

139. Become addicted only to the good things in life (Rom. 12:9).

☆

140. Only travel with people who are going in your direction (Amos 3:3).

☆

141. To avoid being trapped in a bad deal, clarify and verify because some people will cheat and lie (Josh. 9:1-27).

☆

142. Planners can predict their success. Your goal is the destination and your plan is the map to get you there (Luke 14:28-32).

☆

143. Pursuit is the proof of love. If a guy doesn't pursue you, he doesn't love you (Hosea 3:1-3). Hens don't chase roosters!

☆

144. Focus is the secret of the laser beam (1 Kings 13:1-26).

☆

145. Persistence and patience will overcome all obstacles (Luke 18:1-8).

☆

146. Goals are dreams with deadlines (Neh. 6:15-16).

☆

147. It is better to be an amateur of one than a master of none (Exodus 31:1-5).

☆

148. Focus creates energy and momentum (Phil. 3:13).

☆

149. Thought and talk go together like confession and possession (Rom. 10:9-10).

☆

150. Good health is real wealth. Take care of your body and it will take care of you (Rom. 12:1; 1 Cor. 6:16).

☆

151. Education is powerful. The more you know the farther you will go. The more you learn the more you will earn (Prov. 1:5).

152. You can learn from your mistakes or from a mentor. Wise people learn from both. Fools learn from neither (Eccl. 7:5).

153. Grow into your dream daily. Remember it's a process (2 Pet. 3:18; 2 Cor. 3:17-18).

154. The secret of your future is hidden in your daily routine. (Mike Murdock)

156. Make God your invisible partner and you will succeed in all you do in life (Isaiah 41:13).

157. A sky scrapper is built one brick at a time (Neh. 4:6; 6:15-16).

158. Let God turn your scars into stars (2 Cor. 12:7-10; Gal. 6:17).

159. Don't expect little people to understand big ideas (John 2:19-22). You can't put a gallon into a pint.

160. Waiting time is never wasted time if you know what to do in the mean time (Is. 40:30-31; Ps. 27:14).

161. An unproductive day is an unhappy day. When you waste your time, you waste your life (Ps. 118:24).

162. Be kind to father time because he makes no round trips (Ps. 90:12).

☆

163. JOY is spelled Jesus, Others and You (Phil. 2:3-4).

☆

164. Those who obey the higher law of love don't have to worry about the lower law of the land (Rom. 13:10).

☆

165. In matter of principle, stand like a rock; in matter of taste, swim with the current. (Thomas Jefferson)

☆

166. Authority is in place for our protection, provision and promotion. Honor the chain of authority in your life....parents, pastor, police, etc. (Eph. 6:1-4; Heb. 13:17; Rom. 13:1).

☆

167. Every deed begins with a thought. Make sure your thinking is right if you want your behavior to be right (Acts 5:1-5).

☆

168. The purpose of power is to serve. (Martin Luther King, Jr.)

☆

169. A fish wouldn't get caught if he kept his mouth closed. Speech might be silver but silence is golden (Prov. 19:11).

☆

170. Everything is a cinch if you take it by an inch. Everything is hard if you take it by a yard (Exodus 23:29-30).

☆

171. Your eyes are the windows to your soul (Luke 11:34-35).

☆

172. Make smile your style. It's a lot cheaper than plastic surgery and a lot less painful (Neh. 8:10).

☆

173. If you don't want to be forgotten, do something unforgettable (Mark 14:3-9).

☆

174. Knowledge is power only if you know how to use it (2 Kings 5:15-17).

☆

175. Faith is the experiential knowledge of God (Ps. 37:25).

☆

176. Never promise what you cannot deliver (Matt. 26:35).

☆

177. He who talks much does very little (Prov. 14:23).

☆

178. If you want to be successful, always have a good plan and follow it (Prov. 24:3).

☆

179. Never give CPR to something God is killing (1 Sam. 16:1).

☆

180. The greatest person in an organization is the servant of all (Mark 10:43-45). Being a servant keeps your motives pure.

☆

181. The root determines the fruit. If you don't like the fruit, you must change the root (Luke 3:9).

☆

182. To make your life really count, make everyday count. Make everyday your divine masterpiece (Eph. 5:15-17).

☆

183. Discipline is bitter but its fruit is sweet (1 Tim. 4:7-8).

☆

184. A man can climb and fall on the same ladder.
(Booker T. Washington)

☆

185. You are genetically designed and geographically assigned.
You are perfect for your assignment. (Mike Murdock)

☆

186. The only law you have to obey is the law of love
(Matt. 22:36-40). Loving God and others is the essence of life.

☆

187. If you pray, God will show you the way and prepare the way
(Ps. 39:4). He's our Way Maker because He's the Way (John 14:6).

☆

188. Without the grinding wheel the knife remains dull
(Prov. 27:17).

☆

189. Stop working long enough to sharpen your ax (Eccl. 10:10).
Work smarter not harder.

☆

190. Take one day off a week to review, renew and preview the
upcoming week (Exodus 20:8-11).

☆

191. Hard work is the most secure route to success (Deut. 2:7a).
You should get more out of your work than just money.

☆

192. Your attitude will determine your altitude (Phil. 2:5-11).

193. Fully develop yourself for the glory of God and the good of others (1 Cor. 10:31; 2 Tim. 2:20-21).

☆

194. What pains us or shames us often trains us (Ps. 119:71).

☆

195. A small key can unlock big doors if it's the right key (Isaiah 33:6).

☆

196. Whatever you need is already in your life waiting for your recognition (2 Kings 6:1-17).

☆

197. Great people develop and maintain great habits (Dan. 6:11).

☆

198. Everything nice in life has its price (Prov. 6:32-35).

☆

199. You must release it before God will increase it (Mal. 3:8-12).

☆

200. If you increase your giving, God will increase your living (Luke 6:38).

☆

201. The advice you heed will determine the life you lead (Prov. 19:20).

☆

202. What you hear determines what you say (Matt. 12:34b).

☆

203. Your sight will affect your appetite (Job 31:1; Ps. 101:3).

☆

204. Your mouth is a commentary of your mind (Matt. 12:34).

☆

205. Your tongue is connected to your heart (Prov. 4:20-23).

☆

206. To expedite your success, listen more and talk less (Prov. 8:33-34).

☆

207. Your faith schedules your miracles. The sooner you believe the faster you will receive (Mark 11:20-24).

☆

208. There is a big difference between a good idea and a God idea. One originated from below the other from above (James 3:13-18).

☆

209. What God ordains He maintains (Deut. 1:10-11).

☆

210. If you can conceive it in your head, believe it in your heart, you will eventually receive it in your hand (Gen. 37:5-11; 50:20).

☆

211. Mentorship is the fastest route to success. Mentorship is wisdom without the pain of mistakes (Titus 2:1-8).

☆

212. If successful people leave clues, be smart enough to follow them (Rom. 15:4).

☆

213. Tune your instrument before the concert (Mark 1:35).

☆

214. If practice makes perfect, then practice doing it the right way (Acts 18:24-28).

215. Continuous improvement is the key to future success and real security. Never stop growing (1 Pet. 2:2-3; 2 Pet. 3:18).

216. Whatever you expect make sure you inspect. Follow-up is the key to progress and excellence (Acts 15:36-41).

217. As water sinks to its lowest level, so does the person who lacks character (John 18:2).

218. It doesn't do you any good to remove the web if you don't kill the spider (Rom. 7:14-20).

219. Exercise is an easy way to increase the quality and quantity of your life (Josh. 14:10-13).

220. To be balanced you need exercise for your body, education for your mind and worship for your spirit (1 Thes. 5:23).

221. Success is never final; failure is never fatal; it is courage that counts. (Winston Churchill)

222. Get organized at the beginning of the year so that you can thoroughly enjoy the rest of the year (1 Cor. 14:40).

223. You are not assigned to everyone but you have been assigned to someone. Never change who you are to please others (Gal. 1:10).

224. Some will flourish under your leadership while others will flee. You can't lead everybody (John 6:60-69).

☆

225. Care about people, but don't cater to people (John 2:23-25).

☆

226. Do all you can, while you can, as often as you can, as long as you can, for as many people as you can (John 9:4).

☆

227. There are no short cuts to any place worth going in life. (Beverly Sills)

☆

228. The longest distance between two points is a short cut. (John C. Maxwell)

☆

229. Say "no" to the good so you can say "yes" to the best (Phil. 1:9-11).

☆

230. Never take on more than you can prioritize, organize or supervise. If you do, get some qualified help (Exd. 18:1-27).

☆

231. What the devil can't eliminate, he will try to accelerate (Matt. 4:1-11).

☆

232. Whatever you fail to master today, it will master you tomorrow (Judges 16:1-30).

☆

233. What you do habitually you will become permanently. What you do daily is the real you. What you do occasionally is the potential you. Winners do daily what losers do occasionally. (Mike Murdock)

☆

234. The truth will quite often set you on fire before it will set you free (John 8:32).

☆

235. The purpose of discipline is to birth a habit. The purpose of a habit is to create a future. (Mike Murdock)

☆

236. In life you have to do what you have to do in order to get to where you want to go (2 Tim. 2:1-6).

☆

237. Proper preparation prior to preaching will prevent poor performance in the pulpit (2 Tim. 2:15).

☆

238. Always keep your focus on what you're going to and not on what you're going through (Ps. 30:5b; Heb. 12:2).

☆

239. Link your habits to your purpose in life (Luke 4:49; 5:16-19).

☆

240. A man without a smile should not open a shop. (Chinese Proverb)

☆

241. The purpose of your body is to give expression to your soul and spirit (Rom. 12:1-2).

☆

242. The key to making progress in life is to build a perfect day and repeat it (Prov. 4:18). Every day is a new beginning.

☆

243. Develop a rhythm in life by putting your good habits on auto-pilot (Ps. 1:2; 119:164).

☆

244. Take a break before you break. Shut down before you break down (Mark 6:31).

☆

245. Burning the candle at both ends doesn't make you brighter. You just simply burn out faster (Matt. 11:28-30).

☆

246. Your talk reinforces your thoughts. Your talk puts clothes on your thoughts (Matt. 12:34).

☆

247. What you look at the longest will become the strongest (2 Sam. 13:1-13).

☆

248. Only put in your mind the things you want to see happen in time (2 Sam. 11:1-5).

☆

249. Your decisions today will determine your destiny tomorrow (Matt. 7:13-14).

☆

250. Passion is the pathway to your wisdom. Your smartness is revealed in the area of your giftedness (Exd. 31:1-5).

☆

251. If you put God above everything else in life, He will take care of you for the rest of your life (Matt. 6:33).

☆

252. Do right by others and God will do right by you (Eph. 6:7-8).

☆

253. Hard times have a way of bringing people together (2 Kings 7:1-3).

☆

254. Choose your battles carefully. Fighting drains your energy, breaks your focus and uses up your resources (Matt. 5:39-41).

☆

255. Stay humble because God will not let you succeed without Him (1 Pet. 5:5-6).

☆

256. God's greatest gifts often come in plain wrapping (John 1:11). Jesus was born in a manger not in a mansion (Luke 2:1-7).

☆

257. Everything big today started out small yesterday (Job 8:7; Zech. 4:10a).

☆

258. Think big but be willing to start small (Job 8:7; Gen. 12:1-3).

☆

259. A golden connection can change your life forever. Let God connect you to the right people (2 Kings 5:1-3).

☆

260. Vulnerability is a magnet for compassion. Don't be afraid to show people your scars (2 Cor. 12:7-10).

☆

261. Your prayer life reveals your humility or pride. God resists the proud but He gives His grace to the humble (1 Pet. 5:5).

☆

262. Anger is the birth place for change. Nothing happens until somebody gets mad enough to do something (John 2:13-17).

☆

263. Never criticize or condemn what God is blessing. (Rick Warren)

☆

264. The Bible is still the all time best seller because its content is priceless (Ps. 19:10a; 119:127; Prov. 16:16).

☆

265. The Bible is the winner's digest and you don't have to pay for a subscription (Ps. 119:1-176; Ps. 68:11).

☆

266. If you don't live it, you don't believe it. (Paul Harvey)

☆

267. When you increase your wisdom, you will increase your wealth (Prov. 3:15-16).

☆

268. A common enemy unites people (Luke 23:8-12).

☆

269. Make your family your foundation and fountain of inspiration in life (Prov. 5:18).

☆

270. In the long run, usually it's better to give people what you have learned rather than what you have earned (2 Tim. 2:2).

☆

271. Your ability needs responsibility to expose its possibilities. (Theodore Roosevelt)

☆

272. Human potential without godly purpose produces self-destruction. (Myles Munroe)

☆

273. Those who tame lions aren't afraid of dogs (Prov. 28:1).

☆

274. Everything becomes stronger with thought and talk (Gen. 39:6-12).

☆

275. Listen to your enemies for improvement and to your friends for encouragement. (Mike Murdock)

☆

276. Time exposes everything and everybody (John 6:66-70).

☆

277. Starve your weaknesses and feed your strengths (Gal. 5:16).

☆

278. Daily your mind must be renewed and your flesh must be subdued (Rom. 12:1-2; Gal. 5:16).

☆

279. The unwise trust, but the wise test (1 Thes. 5:21).

☆

300. Short term pain is worth long term gain (Heb. 12:7-11).

☆

301. Favor isn't fair. Most things in life aren't (Gen. 37:3-4).

☆

302. Mean bulls make great cowboys. (Barbara A. Kipfer)

☆

303. He who laughs lives long enough to laugh again and again (Prov. 17:22a).

☆

304. Your sight will affect your appetite (Gen. 3:6; Lam. 3:51).

☆

305. People will enter and exit your life for a reason or for a season (Col. 4:14; Philemon 24; 2 Tim. 4:10). Let them come and go.

☆

306. Your wisdom, not your race or gender, will determine your level of success in life more than anything else (Prov. 3:13-16).

☆

307. Your most important mentor is the one you listen to and follow (Prov. 5:1-2). In life, you'll need more than one mentor.

☆

308. Prolonged isolation leads to devastation. Get out and socialize with people often (Ps. 133:1; Heb. 10:25).

☆

309. Life isn't fair, but God is good. Succeed anyhow!
(Robert H. Schuller)

☆

310. In life, aim high! Low ambition is always worse than failure (Phil. 3:14).

☆

311. Learn from those above you, teach those below you, and help those around you. (John C. Maxwell)

☆

312. True success will produce a successor. The organization shouldn't fail after your departure (Josh. 1:1-3).

313. The best way to remember something is to teach it. Repetition is a teacher's best friend (Is. 28:10).

314. When you teach you learn twice. (Barbara A. Kipfer)

315. If you don't go through the process, you won't be able to handle the position once you get the promotion (Gen. 50:20).

316. Bleeding leaders leave a bloody trail because hurting people hurt people (Matt. 2:16-18).

317. Some people are penny wise and dollar dumb. The lowest bid or the cheapest price isn't always the best deal (Matt. 24:24-30).

318. Spend time in His presence before you stand before His people (Matt. 6:6; Acts 4:13; Acts 6:4).

319. You can't have a great public life without a great private life (Mark 1:35; Luke 9:18a).

320. Blessed are the flexible for they shall not be bent out of shape. (Rick Warren)

321. The secrets to living a long life are live right and be nice to people. (Sarah Lewis)

322. The environment you live in will determine your level of growth and character (Ps. 34:1-3; 84:10; 122:1).

☆

323. The quality of your preparation determines the quality of your performance. (Mike Murdock)

☆

324. One miracle can have more impact than a thousand sermons (John 20:30-31).

☆

325. Good words must be backed up with good works (James 1:22).

☆

326. Life is too short for all scores to be settled here on earth (2 Cor. 5:10).

☆

327. The greatest quality of leadership is example (1 Thes. 1:7).

☆

328. God will turn your mess into your message. (Paula White)

☆

329. Talk about your positive expectations rather than your negative experiences (Prov. 18:21).

☆

330. Focus on your opportunities, not your obstacles (Phil. 1:12-18).

☆

331. The seed that leaves your hand never leaves your life but it enters into your future where it multiplies. (Mike Murdock)

☆

332. You can't save time but you can invest it wisely (Eph. 5:18).

☆

333. Busy work isn't the same as productive work (Matt. 7:21-23).

☆

334. When wrong people leave your life, the storm will cease to roar (Jonah 1:4-15).

☆

335. Your hurt today will become someone else's source of healing tomorrow (2 Cor. 1:3-4).

☆

336. You aren't ready to face life until you meet the Author of life (John 10:10b; 17:3).

☆

337. If God wills it, then He'll help you fulfill it (1 John 5:14-15).

☆

338. The Word will work if you work the Word (John 15:7).

☆

339. If you are God's man or woman, then He will give you a command and a plan (Gen. 7:1-5).

☆

340. Your preparation in private will be revealed by your performance in public (2 Tim. 2:15).

☆

341. Great preparation on the front end will ensure great celebration on the latter end (Ezra 6:22).

☆

342. Do not allow yourself to become high and dry. Get the learning but don't lose the burning (Col. 3:16; Eph. 5:18).

☆

343. Fasting and praying forces your flesh to die (Matt. 17:14-21).

☆

344. What you do first determines what God does next
(2 Chron. 7:14).

☆

345. Courage is not the absence of fear. It's faith in the face of fear
(Esther 4:16).

☆

346. You can go anywhere from here if you are willing to take
enough small steps to get there (1 Sam. 3:1-21).

☆

347. Save your prime time for your most important people and
projects (Ps. 5:3; 143:8; Mark 1:35).

☆

348. Watch out for haters. They are vision stealers and dream
killers (Gen. 37:18-20).

☆

349. Hang with people who will support you and not with those
who will sabotage you (Acts 3:1-11).

☆

350. If your best friends are hurricane and tornado, expect to keep
having storms in your life (Prov. 20:3).

☆

351. Always make sure you prepare your people before you
implement any major changes (Luke 24:45-49).

☆

352. Leaders are made in the crucible of suffering (Heb. 5:8).

353. When Satan increases his attacks, you must increase your quiet time (Matt. 26:41-43).

354. Unusual warfare requires unusual weapons--prayer, fasting, fellowship, praise and worship, etc. (2 Cor. 10:3-5).

356. God will often use an enemy to move you to the next season in your life (1 Sam. 17:12-58).

357. Humility is the magnet that attracts God and people (1 Pet. 5:5-6).

358. God gives you tests before He gives you success (Jas. 1:12).

359. The real nature of leadership is sacrifice. The higher you go, the greater the price. (John C. Maxwell)

360. Never use a tank to kill a flea. Make sure the punishment fits the crime (Luke 12:47-48a).

361. You must leave the land of even, before you can get to the land of extra. (Joyce Meyers)

362. Greatness always forces smallness to react (Esther 3:5).

363. Big thinkers intimidate small thinkers (Num. 14:6-9).

364. It takes training, time and trials to grow strong godly leaders (Acts 7:30-34).

☆

365. Your mind has two functions: memory to replay your past victories and imagination to pre-play your future victories (Mike Murdock; See also 1 Sam. 17:34-36).

☆

366. The pain you can feel is the pain you can heal. (Mark 1:40-42).

☆

367. Jesus was never in a hurry. Hurry will only lead to more worry (John 11:4-6).

☆

368. Planning makes you powerful. People follow the man or woman who has a plan (Prov. 14:22).

☆

369. You cannot be a great leader until you first become a great servant because leadership is servant-hood (Mark 10:35-45).

☆

370. You can't lead the crowd and follow it at the same time (Exodus 32:1-35).

☆

371. All of nature is God's art. (Dante)

☆

372. If the people around you don't want to move up, then you need to move on (Matt. 10:14).

☆

373. Pain is the catalyst for change (Luke 15:17-18).

☆

374. The proof of love is the investment of time (Ps. 1:2).

☆

375. Problems and needs create relationships (Matt. 8:5-13).

☆

376. Right person, right place, right plan at the right time equals success (Gal. 4:4).

☆

377. If people speak ill of you, live so that no one will believe them. (Plato)

☆

378. Repentance is the first step towards restoration and reconciliation (2 Chron. 7:14; Prov. 28:13).

☆

379. What you keep is the most it will ever be. What you give is the least it will ever be (Luke 6:38).

☆

380. It's impossible to give anything away because giving always creates a harvest (Eccl. 11:1). If you have a need, plant a seed.

☆

381. Nothing happens until people start talking. And if all they do is talk nothing still will happen (Prov. 14:23).

☆

382. Communication is the life-blood of any organization. You must communicate on all levels--to those above you, below you and on the same level with you (Acts 15:1-35).

☆

383. If you want a big harvest, plant lots of seeds (2 Cor. 9:6). Give regularly, cheerfully, generously and expectantly.

☆

384. Take time to fertilize your own dream before it dies inside of you (Pro. 29:18). Don't die with your dream still inside you.

☆

385. Arrogant people are full of hot air. They are suffering from an acute case of big headedness (Prov. 16:18; 1 Tim. 3:6).

☆

386. Both knowledge and wisdom are progressive because life is intended to be a faith experience (2 Cor. 5:7).

☆

387. Do what you feel in your heart to be right--for you'll be criticized anyway. (Eleanor Roosevelt)

☆

388. Money can't satisfy you (Eccl. 5:10). Only God can satisfy you (Is. 55:1-3). The purpose of money is to meet needs, heal hurts, and solve problems (Eccl. 10:19).

☆

389. Easy come, easy go. People will rarely fight for something that comes easy (Prov. 17:2).

☆

390. When dealing with people, everything must be taught. Don't assume anything (Deut. 6:1-9; 1 Tim. 5:17).

☆

391. If prosperity means being whole, nothing broken, nothing lacking, then I believe in prosperity (Ps. 35:27; 3 John 2).

☆

392. Prosperity simply means having enough of God's provision to fulfill His vision for your life (Ps. 24:1; 84:11; Phil 4:19).

☆

393. Smooth seas do not make skillful sailors. (Africa Proverb)

☆

394. Never worry about your enemy because an enemy exposed can become an enemy defeated (Matt. 26:23).

☆

395. Contentment is a by-product of gratitude (1 Tim. 6:6-8).

☆

396. Disappointment is often God's appointment to get you to your destiny (Gen. 45:4-7).

☆

397. The root of sin is always selfishness. It's placing your will above God's will (1 John 3:4).

☆

398. Prayer is the power that pulls everything together successfully (Phil. 4:6-7). Bathe everything you do in prayer (Luke 18:1).

☆

399. Sin always dishonors God and discredits the leader (Prov. 14:34), but God's grace can give you another chance (1 John 1:9).

☆

400. Stop and smell the roses. Life was meant to be tasted not swallowed (Eccl. 2:24-25).

☆

401. If you continue to sow, eventually your life will kick into overflow (Prov. 3:9-10).

☆

402. Never place your words above God's Word (Prov. 30:5-6).

☆

403. It takes determination and concentration to make it to your destination (Phil. 4:13).

☆

404. Don't mess with the girls or guys, the gold or God's glory. Power, Money and Sex can destroy you (2 Sam. 12:1-14).

☆

405. Resources flow to vision and results. Everyone wants to be on the winning team (Neh. 2:1-9).

☆

406. The Triple C of Success – Character, Competence and Communication are required for success. (John C. Maxwell)

☆

407. Your head may give you direction for the path, but your heart will give you connection with your people (1 Pet. 5:1-4).

☆

408. There is a difference between being broke and being cheap. (Rev. Cato Brooks, Jr.)

☆

409. The biggest room in the world is the room for improvement. (Dennis Kimbro)

☆

410. Courage is a result of conviction (Dan. 3:16-18).

☆

411. Successful people are often envied, hated and misunderstood by unsuccessful people (Matt. 27:18).

412. Where there is life, there is excitement and growth (Acts 2:42-47).

☆

413. Train, explain, and then expect some pain before things will change (Acts 2:36-37).

☆

414. It's easier to give birth than to raise the dead (Gen. 35:16-18).

☆

415. A person or organization is like a shark, it has to keep moving or it will die (2 Thes. 1:3-4).

☆

416. Relationships are the glue that holds an organization together (John 13:34-35).

☆

417. Death is the golden chariot that ushers us into the presence of God. (Tertullian)

☆

418. The strength of an oak tree is its root system (Ps. 1:3). It's what you don't see that counts.

☆

419. Roots grow underground before you see the tree above the ground (Ps. 1:3).

☆

420. Failure is usually a new idea or opportunity in disguise (Rom. 8:28).

☆

421. A problem is often nothing but a blessing in disguise (Gen. 37:36).

☆

422. Success is finding a need and fulfilling it better than anyone else (Acts 10:38).

☆

423. Life is a one way trip. You will not come this way again (Heb. 9:27).

☆

424. Manage your problem until you figure out a way to solve your problem. (John C. Maxwell)

☆

425. Never put a full plate of food in front of a man or woman who isn't hungry (Mark 6:1-6).

☆

426. People who stay in shallow water never learn how to swim or catch big fish (Luke 5:1-11).

☆

427. Success is a two-sided coin; on one side is faith and on the other is work (James 1:20).

☆

428. God only invests in projects that interest Him (Matt. 6:33).

☆

429. Find out what God is blessing and do that. (Rick Warren)

☆

430. Faith enables the believing soul to treat the future as present and the invisible as seen. (J. Oswald Sanders)

☆

431. The best way to help yourself is by helping somebody else (Ps. 112:5).

☆

432. People very seldom do what they are told, but will always do what they see. Be sure to practice what you preach (1 Cor. 11:1).

☆

433. You are what you do regardless of what you say (Matt. 7:17).

☆

434. People might not believe what you say, but they will always believe what you do (1 Thes. 1:7).

☆

435. Sin will make you uncomfortable in the presence of God and godly people (Luke 5:8; Gal. 4:29).

☆

436. What you see and hear determine what you think and feel and what you think and feel will determine what you will say and do (Prov. 6:25).

☆

437. God is against sin because sin is against you (Prov. 13:15).

☆

438. It is never right to do wrong (Prov. 8:13; Rom. 6:23).

☆

439. Always connect with the people before you communicate with them (John 6:1-15).

☆

440. You can't turn a donkey into a race horse no matter how hard you try. Only God can change people (2 Cor. 5:17).

☆

441. Let a challenge stimulate you rather than stop you (1 Sam. 17:1-58).

☆

442. Habit is either the best of servants or the worst of masters. (Nathaniel Emmons)

☆

443. You can't continue to do wrong and finish strong. It's not about how well you start but how well you finish (1 Kings 11:4).

☆

444. Never sacrifice the team for the sake of a player (Josh. 7:1-26).

☆

445. We must keep the message of yesterday while using the methods of today to ensure we will have a future tomorrow. In other words, adapt or die (1 Cor. 9:19-23).

☆

446. Retire from your job but not from life. (Barbara A. Kipfer)

☆

447. Give your best time and effort to your priorities every day (Matt. 6:33; Mark 1:35; Ps. 5:3).

☆

448. Persistence wears down resistance (Luke 18:1-8).

☆

449. A wise person will become a student of successful people and organizations (Prov. 1:5).

☆

450. Be a person of excellence (Dan. 6:3). Don't expect God to bless your mess (1 Cor. 14:40)!

☆

451. Twenty percent of your priorities will give you 80 percent of your production. (Pareto Principle)

☆

452. He who lacks character is morally bankrupt (John 6:70-71).

☆

453. Life cannot always be lived in a major key. On the keyboard of life there are black and white keys. It takes both to play beautiful music (Ps. 137:1-6).

☆

454. You are the answer to somebody's prayers. God will allow you to succeed for the benefit of others (Gen. 50:20).

☆

455. The real definition of leadership is sacrifice. To go higher and farther, it will always cost you more (Luke 22:39-46).

☆

456. Your crisis isn't necessarily my problem. Stay focused, trust God and things will work out (John 11:4-6).

☆

457. Present neglect will lead to future regret (1 Sam. 8:1-3).

☆

458. Get a clue and a bigger view and realize life is never about you (Phil. 2:3). God is concerned about the whole world (Jn 3:16).

☆

459. Since God gave you a brain, make sure you do your own thinking (Prov. 1:10-19).

☆

460. Regardless of how tall your daddy is, you must do your own growing (1 Sam. 8:1-3).

☆

461. Risk takers are willing to go out on a limb because they know that's where the fruit is. (Rick Warren)

☆

462. It's not so much what you eat that will affect your health as what's eating you (Prov. 17:22b).

☆

463. Blessed are the balanced for they shall out last all others. (Bishop T. D. Jakes)

☆

464. If your finger is broken, everything you touch will hurt. (Barbara A. Kipfer)

☆

465. If your foundation is weak, your life will eventually crumble (Matt. 7:24-27).

☆

466. Learn from the past; live in the present; look to the future. God is the only one who isn't affected by time and always remains the same (Mal. 3:6; Heb. 13:8).

☆

467. Purity leads to power and holiness leads to happiness (1 Kings 10:8-9; Ps. 32:2; 2 Cor. 7:1).

☆

468. When the leader is ready, the followers will show up (John 1:35-46).

☆

469. God will allow a series of problems to come your way in order to help your soul grow (Job 42:10; 1 Pet. 5:10).

☆

470. The ultimate purpose of life is the development of the soul and spirit (Rom. 8:28-29).

☆

471. The work you do is a reflection of you (Col. 3:23-24).

☆

472. Behold the turtle; he only makes progress when he sticks his neck out. (Rick Warren)

☆

473. If God gives you an idea, He will make it real (Prov. 8:12).

☆

474. Your dream is God's will for your life (Matt. 1:18-25).

☆

475. A God-given dream will always glorify God and help others (Gen. 50:20).

☆

476. Success and happiness are not matters of chance but choice. (Zig Ziglar)

☆

477. Whether joy or sorrow, this too shall pass (Ps. 30:5b).

☆

478. My organization is a reflection of me, and I must change it if I don't like what I see (Hos. 4:9).

☆

479. If you don't like the crop you're reaping, change the seeds you are sowing (Gal. 6:7).

☆

480. If you don't like the direction of your life is going, change directions (Acts 2:37-40).

☆

481. An unread book can't help you (2 Kings 22:8-13; Hos. 4:6).

☆

482. God will never give you what you refuse to give to another (Luke 6:38).

☆

483. Blessings come from God but through people. God will get it to you if He can get it through you (Gen. 50:20; James 1:17).

☆

484. Make it your life ambition to serve, give and out-love everyone else (1 Cor. 13:13).

☆

485. Planning and preparation will make you powerful and productive (Prov. 6:6-8).

☆

486. Your life today is a reflection of the choices you made yesterday (Prov. 3:5-6).

☆

487. Nothing will ever dominate your life unless it happens daily. (Mike Murdock)

☆

488. Prayer produces joy (Phil. 4:6-7). The Word produces power (Heb. 4:12). You need both to be successful (Acts 6:4).

☆

489. Live locally but think globally (Matt. 28:18-20; Acts 1:8).

☆

490. You can't escape reality but you can help shape it by the power of your faith (Heb. 11:1-6).

☆

491. When you think you know it all, that's all you'll ever know (Prov. 12:1; 13:1).

☆

492. Grace is God's blessing and favor upon your life (Prov. 10:22).

☆

493. Divine promotion is always better than self-promotion or people promotion (Ps. 75:6-7).

☆

494. When you improve yourself, you improve the world (2 Tim. 3:16-17; Eph. 2:10). The world won't get any better unless you do.

☆

495. If you don't take your thoughts captive, they will take you captive (Judges 16:20-22; 2 Cor. 10:3-5).

☆

496. Listen carefully, think twice and speak once (James 1:19-20).

☆

497. The way up is down. The further you go down in service the higher you will go up in honor (Luke 18:13-14).

☆

498. Get up and get out or put up with it and shut up (Prov. 25:24; 27:15)! A good relationship or marriage gets better with time while a bad relationship or marriage gets worse with time.

☆

499. Don't take your blessings for granted; take them with gratitude (Ps. 103:1-3).

☆

500. Education will not only lead to your graduation, but more often than not it will lead to your alienation (John 7:1-5; 10:20).

☆

501. If you are content with your life, you can live with a little or a lot (Phil. 4:11-12).

☆

502. The lead dog has the best view. If you don't like the view, then it may be your turn to become the lead dog (Acts 15:36-41).

☆

503. Your mind is the command and control center of your life (Prov. 7:1-27). What happens in your mind will happen in time.

☆

504. The devil can't do anything to you without your consent and cooperation (James 4:7). You can't resist the devil and entertain him at the same time (1 Pet. 5:8).

☆

505. The persistent person usually wins the prize (Matt. 15:21-31).

☆

506. There isn't any limitation on a person with great faith and a big imagination (Eph. 3:20-21).

☆

507. If you bite off more than you can chew, eventually it will get the best of you (Judges 16:25-31).

☆

508. If people believe in themselves, it's amazing what they can accomplish. (Sam Walton)

☆

509. When you delegate, you allow others to participate (Exd. 18:13-27; Acts 6:1-7).

☆

510. Justice may not be swift but it's always sure. Ultimately, no one ever gets away with anything (Eccl. 12:13-14).

☆

511. I think I have learned that the best way to lift one's self up is to help someone. (Booker T. Washington)

☆

512. Information breeds confidence. Knowledge makes you bold (2 Tim. 2:15; Acts 4:13).

☆

513. If you start seeing a lot of empty seats, then people are voting with their feet (John 6:59-69).

☆

514. Good thoughts produce good things (Phil. 4:8).

☆

515. Without a vision the people perish and without people the vision perishes (Prov. 29:18).

☆

516. There is no poverty that can overtake diligence. (Japanese Proverb)

☆

517. If you can look up, then you can get up (Mark 2:1-12).

☆

518. God builds His kingdom through the local church one soul at a time (Matt. 16:18-19; Acts 2:47b).

☆

519. Successful navigation requires thorough preparation (Ps. 37:5; Prov. 10:4).

☆

520. God is a God of infinite variety. Don't ever try to put God in a box (Gal. 3:26-28). God isn't limited by anyone or anything.

☆

521. Faith and obedience are required for a miracle (Is. 1:19).

☆

522. God blesses those who honor His Word (John 15:7).

☆

523. Those who can't take it won't make it (1 Cor. 15:58).

☆

524. Don't be conned by the conditions around you (Matt. 14:22-33).

☆

525. You must expand your mind before you can expand your life (1 Chron. 4:9-10).

☆

526. Many hands make the load lighter and many heads make the path brighter (Luke 10:1-2).

☆

527. The more you decrease the more God will increase (John 3:30).

☆

528. Order increases your concentration, peace, harmony and productivity (1 Cor. 14:40).

☆

529. Don't let the crowd pull you back into the pack (Gal. 1:11-14).

☆

530. In order to win, you must stay away from sin because sin will do you in (Rom. 6:23). In the end, no one wins who lives in sin.

☆

531. Your outer world is a reflection of your inner world (Prov. 23:7a).

☆

532. The more people you help, the greater your success (Phil. 2:7-11).

☆

533. Don't wait for your ship to come in, go out and meet it (Luke 19:1-10).

☆

534. Think things through then follow things through (Luke 14:28-30).

☆

535. What I can see teaches me a whole lot about the God I cannot see. (Ralph Waldo Emerson)

☆

536. A little bit of guilt will produce a large amount of doubt (Ps. 51:1-13; 1 John 1:9). Confess your sins quickly and move on.

☆

537. Failure is the toll you pay on the road to success. God is a God of a second chance (2 Tim. 4:11).

☆

538. When you make a mistake, your enemies will rub it in but your friends will rub it out (James 5:20).

☆

539. As the family goes, so goes the nation and the world. (Pope John Paul II)

☆

540. Your focus will determine your level of energy (Phil. 4:13).

☆

541. Sometimes you have to deprive yourself of a pleasure to improve your position in life (Dan. 1:8-20).

☆

542. If you don't put a limit on God, He won't put a limit on you (Gen. 18:14; Ps. 78:41-55; Jer. 32:27; Heb. 11:6).

☆

543. The more you complain, the less you'll obtain (Phil. 2:14).

☆

544. If Satan's arsenal of weapons were restricted to a single one, it would be discouragement. (C. S. Lewis)

☆

545. Fix your house before you try to fix the school house, court house, church house or the White House (Josh. 24:15).

☆

546. Two wrongs don't make a right. They just make more trouble for you (Gen. 34:1-31).

☆

547. Integrity needs no defense and worth must be discerned not proven (Luke 23:39-43).

☆

548. Your mind is your gold mine (Prov. 8:12). It is priceless!

☆

549. If you can contain it, then you won't be able to obtain it (Gen. 37:5-11).

☆

550. The collapse of character begins with compromise. (Frederick Douglas)

551. You don't have to be a perfect man in order to be a productive man (Heb. 11:32). God can use you in spite of your flaws.

☆

552. A setback is a set-up for a comeback (Matt. 28:1-6).

☆

553. All behavior is learned---both good and bad (Prov. 22:6).

☆

554. Don't think you are the only cactus in the desert or fish in the sea (Luke 9:49-50).

☆

555. The mind is the measure of a man. (Paul Lawrence Dunbar)

☆

556. Your gifts were given to you by God to glorify Him by serving others (1 Cor. 10:31). Never brag about your gifts!

☆

557. Real security can only be found in God (Rom. 8:35-39).

☆

558. The presence of God is a taste of heaven on earth (Ps. 16:11; Ps. 91:1).

☆

559. Make your quiet time your hour of power (Col. 3:16; Eph. 5:18). It will make the rest of the day more productive.

☆

560. What's the middle letter in Pride? What is the middle letter in Sin? I think you get my point (Prov. 16:18)!

☆

561. When you fail to correct a mistake, you make two mistakes (Prov. 28:13).

☆

562. If life is a game, the Bible is the rule book (Deut. 30:11-16).

☆

563. A dream from God will consume both your mind and time (Gen. 37:5-11; Prov. 29:18).

☆

564. It's impossible to forgive and forget, but it is possible to forgive and move on with your life (Luke 23:34; Eph. 4:31-32).

☆

565. Giving is the highest form of living (Prov. 11:25; Acts 20:35).

☆

566. Faith begins where the will of God is known (Rom. 10:14, 17; Rom. 12:2).

☆

567. It is better to have a piece of a great man than the whole of an average man. (Ruth Graham)

☆

568. Real beauty is soul deep (Prov. 31:30). Focus on the content rather than the container.

☆

569. The only person you have any real control over is you so stop being frustrated by the crazy stuff people do (Prov. 16:32).

☆

570. It's almost impossible to raise whole children in a broken home (Josh. 24:15; Eph. 6:1-4).

☆

571. Hot headed people usually have cold hearts (Prov. 29:22).

☆

572. Being blessed is easy as 1, 2, 3 (Ps. 1:1-3). If you do verses 1 and 2, God will do verse 3. You can't do God's part and He won't do your part. Follow God's formula and you will be blessed.

☆

573. There are three levels of certainty: opinion, belief and conviction (Phil. 1:6; 2 Tim. 1:12).

☆

574. Yesterday is a cancelled check. Tomorrow is a promissory note. Your life is today (Ps. 118:24). Give it all you've got, today!

☆

575. It is easier to slow down a rabbit than to speed up a turtle (Prov. 10:4).

☆

576. If you want to get ahead and stay ahead, then you'll have to keep using your head (Dan. 1:8-20).

☆

577. If you refuse to grow, eventually your life will plateau (Heb. 5:11-14).

☆

578. It's not about how many books you've read, but what kind of life you have led (James 1:22-25).

☆

579. Education is a progressive discovery of our own ignorance. (Will Durant)

☆

580. Books can take you places even when your body is confined to a prison (2 Tim. 4:13).

☆

581. You can do it if you allow God to make you His conduit (Gen. 12:1-3). Become a distribution center for God's blessings.

☆

582. If you live life on the cutting edge, you will always be sharp and ahead of the pack (Prov. 10:4; 12:24; 13:4; 21:5).

☆

583. Be like a postage stamp—stick to one thing until you get there (Phil. 3:13-14).

☆

584. I am because we are. (East Africa Proverb)

☆

585. If you follow-through, eventually you will have a break-through (Luke 8:43-48).

☆

586. To enjoy life, live for eternity rather than for time (Matt. 6:19-21; Phil. 1:21).

☆

587. The orator who wishes to set the people on fire must himself be burning. (Quintillian)

☆

588. All things are created twice, first mentally and then physically (Hab. 2:2-3). If you can see it, you can achieve it.

☆

589. If you can see the invisible, feel the intangible, then you can do the impossible (Mark 11:22-24).

☆

590. Faith comes by hearing and departs when you stop hearing (Rom. 10:17). You must also act on what you hear (Heb. 4:2).

☆

591. Faith keeps the person who keeps the faith. (Mother Teresa)

☆

592. Enjoy the journey and your fellow travelers (Heb. 12:1).

☆

593. It's a sin to be good if God called you to be great.
(Thom S. Rainer)

☆

594. Change your focus and you will change your feeling
(Prov. 23:7a).

☆

595. Organize and prioritize your work for maximum effectiveness
(1 Cor. 14:40).

☆

596. Without enthusiasm there is no progress in the world.
(Woodrow Wilson)

☆

597. There is a difference between success and significance
(Phil. 3:4-7; Heb. 11:23-29).

☆

598. You will never walk on water if you keep sitting in the boat
(Matt. 14:25-33).

☆

599. Bad thoughts and music are junk food for the soul (Phil. 4:8).

☆

600. Don't rock the boat if you aren't going to help row the boat
(Neh. 4:6). Only those who work should add their two cents.

☆

601. Turn your creed into deeds and people will believe
(Matt. 23:1-3).

☆

602. You will have forever the things you give away (Eccl. 11:1).

☆

603. Without rocks and pebbles in the stream, there would be no music (2 Cor. 4:17). No cross, no crown; no pain, no gain.

☆

604. If the sand didn't irritate the oyster, there would be no pearl (1 Pet. 1:6-7).

☆

605. Real success and fulfillment comes from who you are and not from what you have (Luke 12:15).

☆

606. It's the pressure on the coal that produces the diamond (Ps. 119:71). Pressure will make you produce.

☆

607. Following God is more a matter of the heart than the head (Prov. 3:5-6; Rom. 8:14).

☆

608. Stop talking about your mountain and start talking to your mountain (Mark 11:22-24).

☆

609. Real success is based upon the total package (2 Pet. 1:5-9).

☆

610. Sometimes the most godly thing you can do is rest (Mark 6:31). When fatigue walks in, faith walks out. (Mike Murdock)

☆

611. Patience is the queen of all virtues. It can wait while you develop all of the others (James 1:2-4).

☆

612. Envy shoots at others and wounds itself. (Swedish Proverb)

☆

613. If you have everything you need, and some of the things you want, stop complaining and be happy (1 Tim. 6:6-8; Heb. 13:5-6).

☆

614. Don't spend your future in order to enjoy the present (Prov. 22:7). When you buy what you don't need you steal from yourself.

☆

615. Become a life-long learner (Matt. 11:28-30). When you stop learning and growing, you die from the neck up (1 Tim. 5:6).

☆

616. If you have to spoil someone, spoil your spouse not your children (Eph. 5:21-33).

☆

617. Excellence is doing your very best every time (Gal. 6:4).

☆

618. Truth out of balance is error (Acts 20:25-31).

☆

619. Insecure people indoctrinate. Secure people educate (Matt. 11:28-30). That's the difference between a cult and a real church.

☆

620. Faith can't operate where the will of God isn't known (Hosea 4:6; Matt. 11:1-6).

☆

621. A lesson from the journey of life is, expect delays (Acts 14:21-22).

☆

622. Success or failure starts and ends with you (Phil. 4:8).

☆

623. Attitude always determines altitude (Phil. 4:13).

☆

624. Intuition is often God talking to us (1 Kings 19:1-13).

☆

625. Intuition is nothing but facts buried below the sub-conscious level (Ps. 46:10).

☆

626. You cannot put straight in others what is warped in yourself. (Athanasius)

☆

627. God doesn't have any grandchildren in his family--only sons and daughters (John 3:1-8).

☆

628. Tithing (10%) is kingdom taxation. An offering (anything above 10%) is kingdom investing. (Miles Munroe)

☆

629. DEBT is **D**oing **E**verything **B**ut **T**ithing (Hag. 1:6).

☆

630. Nothing is ever achieved until someone believes (Matt. 9:27-31; Heb. 11:6).

☆

631. Only God can make you the leader of the people in their hearts (Acts 13:22).

☆

632. Turn every test into a testimony (John 9:1-25).

☆

633. Thinking is the process of asking and answering questions and seeing things from a different perspective (Matt. 22:41-45).

☆

634. Humility is the ability to keep learning and growing (Matt. 11:28-30).

☆

635. Continuous growth requires change (Rom. 12:2).

☆

636. Survival depends on your ability to adapt (Luke 5:36-39).

☆

637. You will never be last if you put God first (Matt. 19:27-30).

☆

638. Broad leadership is built on deep character (Ruth 3:11; 4:13-22).

☆

639. Each organization is a reflection of its leader (Hos. 4:9).

☆

640. A little wisdom can obtain a lot of wealth (Prov. 8:18).

☆

641. If you have strong faith, nothing is impossible for you (Mark 9:23).

☆

642. Nurture and cherish your dream until it becomes a reality (Gen. 40:12-15).

☆

643. Every great achievement begins as a dream (Gen. 37:5-11).

☆

644. Leaders are self-motivated people (Acts 14:19-22).

☆

645. The opposite of greed is contentment (1 Tim. 6:6-8).

☆

646. When you forgive others you set yourself free
(Matt. 6:14-15).

☆

647. Be content where you are until God takes you to where you
want to be (Heb. 13:5).

☆

648. The greatest discovery you'll ever make is the will of God
for your life. The greatest achievement is to do the will of God.
Success then is knowing and doing the will of God. (Ron Hart)

☆

649. Want power is will power in action (Phil. 2:13).

☆

650. I would rather attempt to do something great and fail than to
do nothing and succeed. (Robert H. Schuller)

☆

651. The ruin of a nation begins in the homes of its people.
(West Africa Proverb)

☆

652. Those who wait for their ship to come in will realize that its
name is hardship (Prov. 24:33-34).

☆

653. Without the potter, clay is just useless dirt (Jer. 18:1-6).

☆

654. Prayer changes cowards into conquerors (Acts 4:31).

☆

655. It takes a whole lot of faith to believe in nothing. An atheist is a faithless theologian (Ps. 14:1; 55:1).

☆

656. Wisdom gives wings to knowledge like wind gives flight to a kite (Prov. 2:1-6).

☆

657. Wisdom is the proper application of knowledge (Prov. 2:1-6).

☆

658. Build on your strengths and compensate for your weaknesses (Gal. 2:7-8).

☆

659. Never make an important decision when you are tired because tried eyes can't see clearly or accurately (1 Kings 19:1-6).

☆

660. Prolonged pain often brings about a change (Ps. 119:71).

☆

661. Today's thoughts and actions will define your tomorrows (Prov. 23:7a).

☆

662. Never assume a tree is dead in the winter. Wait until spring and it might sprout again (Acts 14:19-20).

☆

663. Your life today is the result of your choices you made yesterday (Deut. 30:19-20).

☆

664. Example is not the main thing in influencing others. It is the only thing. (Albert Schweitzer)

☆

665. If your thoughts run your life, make sure you send them where you want to go (Phil. 4:8).

☆

666. Turn your cares into prayers (Phil. 4:6-7).

☆

667. Where there is no involvement, there is no commitment (Luke 14:16-27).

☆

668. When you improve your world you improve the world (2 Pet. 3:18).

☆

669. Whatever is worth doing at all is worth doing well. (Philip Chesterfield)

☆

670. Success is achieved one day at a time (Prov. 4:18).

☆

671. Relationship must come before rules (Mark 2:27).

☆

672. Men are alike in their natures; it is their habits that separate them. (Confucius)

☆

673. Fear attracts attack. Don't go through life with a victim's mentality (James 4:7).

☆

674. Each victory authorizes God to promote you (1 John 5:3-5).

☆

675. Imagination is more powerful than knowledge. (Albert Einstein)

☆

676. The best way out is always through (Isaiah 43:2).

☆

677. The key to success is focus (Phil. 3:13).

☆

678. The key to failure is broken focus (2 Tim. 4:9-10).

☆

679. Time is renewable. Every day is a new beginning (Ps. 118:24; Lam 3:23).

☆

680. The best way to predict the future is to create it. (Peter Drucker)

☆

681. Always replace a bad habit with a good habit (John 8:1-11).

☆

682. Don't go through life talking about what you could have done or should have done; the point is you didn't (Phil. 3:13-14).

☆

683. Real worship gives us a glimpse of heaven (Gen. 5:4).

☆

684. Ignorance creates a whole host of other negative consequences (Hos. 4:6).

☆

685. Words and images create pictures in your mind. Your mind is your mental TV. You can change the channel if you don't like what you see (Ps. 101:3).

☆

686. Read today, lead tomorrow (2 Tim. 3:16-17).

☆

687. It's better to do something imperfectly than to do nothing perfectly (Prov. 24:16).

☆

688. Habits are formed through discipline (Prov. 6:23).

☆

689. The goal of life is to become Christ-like (Gal. 4:19).

☆

690. Beginning is half done (Luke 2:15).

☆

691. Be wise and help those who have gone astray find their way (Prov. 11:30; Dan 12:3).

☆

692. You friends are a reflection of you (Prov. 13:20).

☆

693. Ninety-nine percent of failure comes from people who have the habit of making excuses. (George Washington Carver)

☆

694. Order is doing the right thing at the right time in the right place with the right people (1 Cor. 14:40).

☆

695. Your daily habits are creating an irreversible future (Gal. 6:7).

☆

696. Nothing succeeds like success because success breeds success (Matt. 19:1-2; 20:29).

697. God can accomplish in 5 minutes what we can't do in 5 years (Luke 13:10-13).

698. People who take care with them never really go any place worth going (Phil. 4:6-7).

699. To keep moving forward in life, you must learn, commit and do (Rom 12:1-2).

700. Some people freeze in winter while others ski. (Barbara A. Kipfer)

701. Life has its seasons. Know the season you're in (Eccl. 3:1-8).

702. Find out which way God is going and go that way (Prov. 3:5-6; Rom. 8:14).

703. Leaders are lifters. The more people you lift the higher you will go (Mark 9:32-35).

704. If you don't believe you can do it, no one else will (Phil. 4:13).

705. Let your goals guide you (Heb. 12:2; Phil. 3:10-11).

706. The old remind us of the past and the young bring us the future. We need both for balance (Prov. 20:29).

707. A little is a lot if it's enough (1 Kings 17:1-16).

☆

708. Adopt a "people first" policy. People are your only appreciable asset (1 Cor. 9:19-23).

☆

709. Learning today prepares you for the future (2 Tim. 2:15).

☆

710. A small leak will sink a large ship (1 Cor. 5:6; Eccl. 9:18).

☆

711. All behavior is belief driven. In order to change your behavior, you must first change what you believe (Rom. 12:2).

☆

712. At death a believer goes from being a caterpillar to a butterfly (1 John 3:2).

☆

713. Death is the beginning of a whole new life (Phil. 1:21).

☆

714. Character is usually home grown (Prov. 22:6; Eph. 6:1-4).

☆

715. The successful are tested within the furnace of adversity (1 Pet. 4:12-16).

☆

716. Look at the man in the mirror because you can only rise and achieve to the level of your self-image (2 Kings 13:15-16).

☆

717. Happy people are usually the healthiest people (Prov. 15:13; 15:15; 17:22).

☆

718. Whatever dominates your mind will dominate your mouth (Matt. 12:34).

☆

719. The difference between success and failure is preparation (Mal. 3:1; Matt. 3:3).

☆

720. When you are ready, people and opportunities will find you (Gen. 41:1-43).

☆

721. You shouldn't be jealous of anybody because nobody has everything and everybody has something. (Dr. Caesar W. Clark)

☆

722. Wealth and power follows the numbers (Luke 8:1-3).

☆

723. A problem is a call to action (Neh. 1:1-11).

☆

724. Everything starts at home….good or bad (Prov. 22:6).

☆

725. When you look at a child you are looking at the future (Is. 9:6; Luke 2:25-32).

☆

726. Strength comes from commitment. Once you make the commitment the strength will come (Gal. 2:20).

☆

727. Little people belittle other people. Big people build others up (1 Thes. 5:14-15).

☆

728. Little people discuss people, average people discuss events, but great people discuss ideas. (Barbara A. Kipfer)

☆

729. Why be a cheap copy when you can be a genuine original (John 7:40-46).

☆

730. The best way to keep a secret is to keep it to yourself (Prov. 20:19).

☆

731. The person with a dream is more powerful than the man with all the facts (Gen. 37:5-11).

☆

732. How you spend your time is how you spend your life (Eph. 5:15-16).

☆

733. When you waste your time you waste your life (Ps. 90:12).

☆

734. An investment in knowledge pays great interest. (Benjamin Franklin)

☆

735. If life is tough, then you must be tougher (1 Pet. 5:10).

☆

736. Weekends should be for your family and your faith (Exodus 20:8-11).

☆

737. If you fall down 7 times, then get up 8 (Prov. 24:15-16).

☆

738. Always begin with the end in mind (Is. 46:10).

☆

739. You were born for greatness. Don't die average (Eph. 3:20-21).

☆

740. You do not test the resources of God until you try the impossible. (F. B. Meyer)

☆

741. Learn to triumph over your trouble (1 Cor. 15:57-58).

☆

742. Knowing how to benefit from failure is the key to success. (Zip Ziglar)

☆

743. A lie is short lived. A half-truth is a whole lie (Prov. 17:4).

☆

744. In a moral universe no one gets away with anything (Num. 32:23).

☆

745. Focus on God's promises instead of your pain (Heb. 12:2).

☆

746. Faith gives us living joy and dying rest. (D. L. Moody)

☆

747. The most powerful force is the world is a positive idea in the mind of a believer who is walking in God's will. (Robert H. Schuller)

☆

748. Always stay in the center of God's will for your life (Rom. 12:2; 1 Thes. 4:3; 1 Thes. 5:18).

☆

749. People judge you by your actions, not by your intentions (Luke 6:43-44a).

☆

750. The education of a man is never completed until he dies.
(Robert E. Lee)

☆

751. People can't find happiness because it has never been lost. It's a by-product of fulfilling one's purpose in life (Heb. 12:2).

☆

752. When you worry about yesterday or tomorrow, you steal from today (Matt. 6:34).

☆

753. You must be able to read the people before you can lead the people (1 Chron. 12:32).

☆

754. Discern the situation before you head into action
(1 Chron. 12:32).

☆

755. Faith puts God between us and our circumstances.
(Daniel Webster)

☆

756. Become a principle-centered person (Prov. 4:7).

☆

757. Worry is nothing but unbelief in disguise (Matt. 8:23-27).

☆

758. Morality is the cement that holds society together
(Prov. 11:11; 14:34).

☆

759. He who provide for this life but takes not care for eternity, is wise for a moment but a fool forever. (Tilleston)

760. Never be afraid to pursue your dreams (Ps. 27:1).

☆

761. Rise above your circumstances (2 Cor. 5:7; Phil. 4:13).

☆

762. Life is fragile. Handle it with prayer (James 5:17-18).

☆

763. Everything can be improved and made better (Phil. 3:14).

☆

764. Strive for improvement not perfection (Phil. 3:13).

☆

765. Courage has no greater ally than preparation (2 Tim. 2:15).

☆

766. A seed is a tiny beginning with a huge future
(Matt. 13:31-32). You are a walking warehouse of seeds.

☆

767. Live with an attitude of gratitude because the world owes you
nothing (1 Thes. 5:18).

☆

768. Be curious and life will become an unending study of joy and
excitement (Eccl. 5:18).

☆

769. The most valuable and dangerous thing in the world is an idea
acted upon (Deut. 1:21-26).

☆

770. Trusting God will give you courage to put your idea into
action (1 John 5:14-15).

☆

771. The secret of excellence is concentration (Dan. 6:3).

☆

772. A divided mind is a weak mind (James 1:8).

☆

773. Winning in the game of life authorizes God to promote you (1 John 5:5).

☆

774. Plan your time wisely and stick with your plan (Prov. 6:6-8).

☆

775. A plan gives you direction and focus (Rom. 15:24).

☆

776. Your dream will give you energy. If your dream no longer motivates you, get a new dream (Gen. 37:5-11).

☆

777. If you have the faith, God's got the power (Matt. 17:20).

☆

778. Indecision saps energy, so make up your mind and stop wasting time (James 1:8).

☆

779. Godly behavior is proof of wisdom (Matt. 11:19).

☆

780. Order is the proper arrangement of things. Have a place for everything and put everything in its place (1 Cor. 14:40).

☆

781. Hope-filled thinking produces enormous energy (Heb. 6:19).

☆

782. Every decision you make affects your character (Prov. 3:5-6).

☆

783. You become the person you are by your daily actions (Duet. 30:19-20).

☆

784. Discipline yourself to seek God every day and you will have a great life (Ps. 42:1-2).

☆

785. If you can see it, you can seize it (Mark 11:22-24; Num. 13:30).

☆

786. You are what you think habitually (Prov. 23:7a).

☆

787. If it grows up over night, it can blow up over night (2 Pet. 3:18).

☆

788. Successful people live disciplined lives (1 Cor. 9:24-27).

☆

789. Evaluation prevents stagnation and exaggeration (2 Cor. 5:10).

☆

790. Be more interested in service and significance than in success and security (Acts 20:24).

☆

791. He lives long who lives well (Eph. 6:1-3).

☆

792. Science is God giving man a peak into His creation (Ps. 19:1-5).

☆

793. We may let God down, but He'll never let us down
(2 Tim. 2:13).

☆

794. Whatever you have done successfully, you can do it again
(Job 42:10).

☆

795. Success formula: I believe, I act and I will succeed
(2 Cor. 5:7).

☆

796. To go far in life, you must row your own boat (Phil. 4:13).

☆

797. Take the word impossible out of your vocabulary (Mark 9:23).

☆

798. Be ruthless with distractions by protecting your focus
(Josh. 1:6-7).

☆

799. The size of your seed will determine the size of your harvest
(2 Cor. 9:6).

☆

800. Everyone must start somewhere. Bloom where you are
planted (1 Cor. 7:20).

☆

801. Use what you have and more will be given when you need it
(Matt. 14:17-21).

☆

802. Do not expect to receive from others what you have not given
(Luke 6:38).

☆

803. Giving is the secret to living. The more you give the more you live (Acts 20:35).

☆

804. Don't expect to find old heads on young shoulders (Prov. 20:29). Wisdom usually comes with time and experience.

☆

805. God will never ask you to sin for His sake (1 Pet. 1:16).

☆

806. Victory comes from obeying God's Word regardless of how you feel (Duet 28:1-14; Is. 1:19).

☆

807. Anytime you do wrong you create a crack in the moral foundation of your character (Gen. 3:8-11).

☆

808. The most important day in your life is today (Ps. 118:24; Matt. 6:34).

☆

809. For neither God nor man can use a discouraged soul. (A. W. Tozer)

☆

810. The size of man is measured by what it takes to discourage him. (Jerry Falwell)

☆

811. Satan's most lethal arrows are doubt and discouragement. (John MacArthur)

☆

812. Be a slave only to your conscience. Let your conscience be your guide and not the opinions of others (Rom. 14:23).

☆

813. Anything you give your attention to, you will do well (Eccl. 9:10).

☆

814. Respect is earned on difficult ground. (John C. Maxwell)

☆

815. Investigate before you invest (Matt. 10:16).

☆

816. We are in bondage to the law in order that we may be free. (Cicero)

☆

817. Genius is 1 percent inspiration and 99 percent perspiration. (Thomas A. Edison)

☆

818. We can always find time to do what is important to us (Phil. 4:13).

☆

819. Big things happen to big thinking people (1 Chron. 4:9-10).

☆

820. The morals of a nation are found in its music (Ps. 137:1-4).

☆

821. Music tells us about the time in which we live (Exodus 15:1-2).

☆

822. Life is what you make it, and how you take it (2 Tim. 4:5; 1 Pet. 2:20-21).

☆

823. Make a decision and then manage your decision to the end (Josh. 24:15).

☆

824. Your action will always speak louder than your words (2 Kings 17:15).

☆

825. The difference in people is how they think (Num. 13:33).

☆

826. To succeed in life get started early and never quit (Luke 2:48-52).

☆

827. Winners never quit and quitters never win (1 Cor. 15:58).

☆

828. Regardless of what happens to you in life, keep working on your dream (Gal. 6:9).

☆

829. A crisis will reveal who your real friends are (Matt. 26:56).

☆

830. Richness is measured by the depth of your relationship with God and others (Luke 12:16-21).

☆

831. Obedience is faith in action (Luke 7:1-10).

☆

832. Sometimes we have to face the music even though we may not like the tune (2 Sam. 12:1-14).

☆

833. I have the power to choose my response in any given situation. Event plus my Response will determine my Outcome. (E. Clement Stone)

☆

834. Hell is full of people who rejected correction (Luke 13:1-5).

☆

835. God created the Devil so that we might have a choice (Duet. 30:15). Then God goes out of His way to save us (2 Pet. 3:9).

☆

836. Hell was not prepared for people but for the devil and his demons. Never go where you are not welcomed (Matt. 25:41).

☆

837. Until you master yourself, you will never master anything else (2 Tim. 2:20-22).

☆

838. You must master your habits, mind, and emotions daily (Ps. 5:3; Mark 1:35).

☆

839. God can always afford to do what He wants done (Gen. 18:14; Phil. 4:19).

☆

840. Always keep your word. If you can't for some reason, notify the person (1 Thes. 2:17-18). You are no better than your word.

☆

841. God delays are not God denials (Hab. 2:2-3).

☆

842. Do not buy what you cannot afford (Heb. 13:5; Phil. 4:11-12).

☆

843. Joy is proof of God's presence (Ps. 16:11b).

☆

844. Visualize and verbalize your goals daily. The ultimate goal of life is God (Gen. 12:1-3; 15:1-5). This is the secret to happiness.

☆

845. Your words are your faith or doubt speaking (Gen. 18:9-15).

☆

846. Don't let your gifts take you where your character can't keep you (1 Sam. 15:24-26).

☆

847. Faith makes the impossible possible (Rom. 4:17-21).

☆

848. If you are not expandable, you will become expendable (Matt. 9:16-17).

☆

849. When I get my thinking, believing, speaking, and actions right, my life will get right (Duet. 6:5; Col. 3:16; Rom. 12:2).

☆

850. If you want to be great, then read biographies of great people, and do what they did (Heb. 11:1-40).

☆

851. Praying and fasting will sharpen your focus and sensitivity to the Holy Spirit (Mark 9:29).

☆

852. Your goals will keep you growing and going. Never stop dreaming (Phil. 3:14).

☆

853. Don't stop at the top. Find another mountain to climb. (Robert H. Schuller)

☆

854. Use your success as a platform to bless others (Gen. 12:1-3).

☆

855. Satisfied needs do not motivate (Amos 6:1).

☆

856. Negative and pessimistic people suffer from an acute case of mental illness (Phil. 4:8).

☆

857. If you can control your mouth, you can control your life (James 3:2).

☆

858. The quality of your life is based upon the well being of your soul (3 John 2).

☆

859. Adversity is a great teacher (Ps. 119:71).

☆

860. Principles are proven guidelines for human behavior (Prov. 4:7).

☆

861. If I had only three remaining years of ministry, I would spend two of them studying. (Donald Grey Barnhouse)

☆

862. Develop yourself to your fullest potential (1 Cor. 13:11).

☆

863. You must fear less in order to achieve more (2 Tim. 1:7).

☆

864. The sum total of goodness equals greatness (Gal. 5:22-23).

☆

865. God put the letter B in the word beginning back before the beginning ever began to be (Gen. 1:1; Rev. 1:8).

866. Read, learn, and grow and then put your wisdom in a book and sell it to the world (Ps. 68:11).

867. It's not about what happens to you, but what happens in you (Gen. 50:20).

868. It's not what happens to us, but our response that hurts us (Gen. 50:20).

869. Weak people use strong words. Don't use profanity nor be entertained by it (Eph. 4:29).

870. What you sow today you will reap tomorrow (2 Cor. 9:6). Learn to sow, wait, and then reap.

871. Say no to the status quo (2 Cor. 8:7). Strive for excellence!

872. Sin always takes you out of the garden and puts you in the wilderness (Gen. 3:23-24).

873. To live is to grow. And to grow is to get old. And to get old is to die. This is called "the circle of life" (1 Tim. 6:7).

874. A bold attempt is success (Prov. 28:1; Ps. 27:1-3).

875. A big shot is a little shot that kept on shooting. (John C. Maxwell)

☆

876. A man's belief system will determine his conduct and character (Gen. 18:17-19).

☆

877. Let us come together and do collectively what we can't do individually. (Pastor D. Grady Scott)

☆

878. Wisdom and knowledge are the twins of success (2 Chron. 1:10).

☆

879. Failure is better than low ambition (Matt. 14:25-33).

☆

880. A church is a religious support group (1 John 3:11).

☆

881. The church is a hospital for the sinners not a museum for saints (Matt. 9:10-13).

☆

882. Growth demands a temporary surrender of security. (Gail Sheehy)

☆

883. Make sure a request is legit before you commit (Acts 9:10-22).

☆

884. Action is the best cure for worry (1 Cor. 15:58).

☆

885. Reputation is who others think you are. Character is who you really are (Prov. 22:1).

☆

886. If you take care of your character in private, you won't have to worry about your reputation in public (Gal. 5:16).

887. Who you are in the dark, when no one is looking, is the real you (Ps. 90:8).

888. Trust must be earned not given (Acts 9:26; 15:1-35).

889. Don't let your rules rule you. Lighten up (Matt. 12:1-13).

890. A true friend steps in when everybody else steps out (Acts 9:23-27).

891. A real friend knows all about you and still loves you (Prov. 17:27).

892. You were created by a great God to do great things with your life (Ps. 48:1-14).

893. To win in the game of life, you must play the hand you're dealt skillfully (Eccl. 10:10).

894. Man can give us knowledge but only God can give us wisdom (James 1:5). Knowledge is plentiful but wisdom is very rare.

895. Be all you can be. God's gift to you is your potential. Reaching your full potential is your gift to God (Matt. 25:14-30).

896. There is a light behind every shadow. Likewise, God is behind every event in your life working all things for your good and His glory (Rom. 8:28).

☆

897. The moon has no light of its own. The moon gets it light from the sun. Apart from God, you have no light (John 8:12).

☆

898. Do what you are gifted to do. If your mama said you can sing, then that doesn't count (1 Cor. 7:7).

☆

899. Take care of the golden goose and you'll always have golden eggs (2 Chron. 20:20b; 1 Cor. 9:7-11; 1 Tim. 5:17-18).

☆

900. It doesn't do you any good to read the Bible if you don't plan to heed it (Luke 6:46; James 1:22).

☆

901. If you take care of God's business, He will take care of your business (Matt. 6:33).

☆

902. Your life is your sermon (2 Cor. 3:2).

☆

903. People would rather see a sermon than to hear one any day (1 Thes. 1:7).

☆

904. What you see is what you get. The "me" I see is the "me" I'll be (Num. 13:33).

☆

905. Until you believe it, you will never achieve it (Matt. 9:29).

906. A big problem is a little problem that was never handled (2 Chron. 36:15-16).

907. The size of the dream will determine the size of the dreamer (Gen. 17:5-8).

908. The difference between people is their dream (Gen. 37:5-11).

909. Excellence is the motto of great achievers (Dan. 6:3).

910. One man's problem is another man's opportunity (1 Sam. 17:4-51).

911. It takes both rain and sunshine to make a rainbow (Rom. 8:28).

912. Uncertainty adds excitement to life (2 Cor. 5:7).

913. Ignorance enslaves the soul (Hos. 4:6).

914. Most people are tuned to WIIFM -- **What's In It For Me** (Matt. 20:20-21; Mark 10:28-30).

915. It takes guts to get off your butt and leave your rut (2 Kings 7:1-4).

916. In life, everything changes except for God (Mal. 3:6).

917. He who sows barley will not gather wheat. You can only reap what you sow (Gal. 6:7).

☆

918. God's presence ensures His blessings (1 Chron. 13:12-14).

☆

919. Tithing is the floor, not the ceiling. Never brag about giving God a dime (Ps. 116:12). Be a grace giver and go beyond 10%.

☆

920. The best luck in the world is to get up off of your butt and do something with your life (Prov. 6:9-11).

☆

921. The most important people in your life are your family (1 Tim. 3:4-5).

☆

922. Your spouse should be your partner and best friend in life (Gen. 2:18; Heb. 13:4). Don't confide in the opposite sex.

☆

923. Giving is investing with God (Eccl. 11:1; Luke 6:38).

☆

924. Marriage is a joint-venture and partnership (Matt. 19:4-6).

☆

925. Turn every negative experience into a positive venture (Gen. 50:20).

☆

926. Great things take time. Rome wasn't built in a day (John 2:20-22).

☆

927. Self-centered people are off-centered (Mark 10:35-45).

☆

928. Life on earth in the beginning of eternity (John 14:1-3).

☆

929. Hope is a perfect life preserver in the midst of a storm (Heb. 6:19).

☆

930. Wanting more is the first step to getting more (1 Chron. 4:9-10).

☆

931. A great man shows his greatness by the way he treats little men. (Thomas Carlyle)

☆

932. Be ashamed to die until you have done something for humanity. (General Douglas MacArthur)

☆

933. Your quiet time should serve as your well of motivation (Mark 1:35).

☆

934. Be an initiator of good and an imitator of God (1 Cor. 11:1).

☆

935. Negative and pessimistic people have a mental health problem (Phil. 4:8). They are victims of fear, worry and doubt.

☆

936. You will learn more from your failures than your successes (Heb. 5:8; 2 Cor. 12:7-10).

☆

937. Power that comes too easily and too fast corrupts (1 Tim. 3:6-7).

☆

938. In life, you will usually get what you expect (Matt. 9:29).

☆

939. If you get the first half of your life right, the second half will take care of itself (Eph. 6:1-4).

☆

940. Live by the 80/10/10 rule. Give God 10%. Save or invest 10%. Live on the other 80% (Prov. 3:9-10; Mal. 3:8-10).

☆

941. There are three stages to life: learning, earning and returning. (Author Unknown)

☆

942. Every experience can teach you a valuable lesson (Phil. 4:11-12).

☆

943. You can learn something from anybody (Is. 11:6).

☆

944. Always give people room to repent and save face (James 2:12-13).

☆

945. You have to step out in order to find out (Matt. 14:25-33).

☆

946. Make your future larger than your past (Josh. 14:1-12).

☆

947. Anyone or anything that decreases your desire for God is your real enemy (Matt. 5:29-30). Avoid them like the plague.

☆

948. The world stands aside to let anyone pass who knows where he is going. (David Starr Jordon)

☆

949. When you fight fire with fire you leave behind a whole lot of ashes. Instead, always overcome evil with good (Rom. 12:21).

☆

950. Most people don't need a face lift. They need a faith lift (Ps. 121:1-2).

☆

951. In life hope is essential to cope. "Leaders are dealers of hope". (Napoleon)

☆

952. Each victory is a step up the ladder of success (1 Sam. 17:34-37).

☆

953. When you expand your knowledge, you expand your world (Luke 2:40; 52).

☆

954. Wealth consists in not having great possessions but in having few wants. (Epicurus)

☆

955. Faith will cure your bouts with doubts (Rom. 10:17).

☆

956. Know thyself and to your own self be true (Rom. 7:18).

☆

957. Do something with your life that will outlive you by investing in people (2 Tim. 2:2).

☆

958. God has given you everything you need to succeed (Phil. 4:19).

☆

959. Tomorrow's provision will not come today (Ps. 68:19).

☆

960. He who ceases to be better ceases to be good.
(Oliver Cronwell)

☆

961. Only those who know the way can show the way
(John 14:1-6).

☆

962. If you know the way, then go the way (Exodus 18:20).

☆

963. We see everything through the tinted glasses of our attitude
(Prov. 23:7a).

☆

964. The seed determines the fruit, not the soil (James 3:12a).

☆

965. A person's worth cannot be measured by a test but by Calvary
(Matt. 12:12; John 3:16).

☆

966. If it was easy to be successful, then everyone would be
successful (Prov. 10:4).

☆

967. If you follow the crowd, you will get lost in it
(Matt. 26:58-75).

☆

968. You were created by God for God (Col. 1:16).

☆

969. You must have long-range goals to keep you from being
frustrated by short-range failures. (Charles C. Noble)

☆

970. If you can fix your head, you can fix your life (Rom. 12:2).

☆

971. Power is the ability to accomplish a goal (Matt. 28:18-20; Luke 10:19; Acts 1:8).

☆

972. Measure a man by his faith and imagination not his intellect (1 Cor. 2:4-5).

☆

973. Wealth needs wisdom to guide it (1 Kings 3:5-14).

☆

974. The most pathetic person in the world is a person with sight and no vision. (Helen Keller)

☆

975. If you increase your level of giving, God will increase your standard of living (Luke 6:38).

☆

976. Children act in public like they act at home (Prov. 22:6).

☆

977. The unexamined life is not worth living. (Plato)

☆

978. He climbs highest who helps another up (Acts 3:1-18).

☆

979. Every ending is a new beginning. Death is the prelude to eternity (Rev. 21:1-5).

☆

980. In life keep moving boldly, bravely, upward, onward and forward (Phil. 3:14).

☆

981. At the core of faith is commitment (Luke 9:23).

☆

982. Pioneers, trail blazers and mavericks ensure our survival and bring us the future (2 Cor. 11:23-28).

☆

983. Take the road not traveled and make a trail (Matt. 7:13-14).

☆

984. Relaxation permits creativity. Find a place to think your thoughts (2 Kings 4:8-11).

☆

985. Nature relaxes the souls. Enjoy a sunset or a walk in the park (Ps. 23:1-6). Remember that God is with you as you walk along.

☆

986. Observation of nature should make it easy to believe in God (Ps. 19:1-3).

☆

987. It's not a sin to be wealthy, but it is a sin be stingy and selfish (1 Tim. 6:17-19).

☆

988. To go higher in life, raise your expectation level (Matt. 9:29).

☆

989. The greatest weapons on earth are God's Word and our words (Ps. 107:20; James 3:5).

☆

990. Tradition is the living faith of those now dead. Traditionalism is the dead faith of those now living. (Author Unknown)

☆

991. A want is something you desire but a need is something you can't do without (Phil. 4:19). Know the difference!

☆

992. Criticism is usually the opinion of a loser or negative person (2 Sam. 16:1-12). No one build monuments to critics.

☆

993. What people think of you is none of your business. God's opinion of you is the only one that really matters (Col. 3:17).

☆

994. Stay calm and you'll do no harm (James 1:19-20).

☆

995. Be a tomorrow-thinker. Don't live just for today (1 Cor. 15:19).

☆

996. Don't play the blame game. Take 100 percent responsibility for your life (Gen. 3:8-13). You have the ability to respond.

☆

997. No matter how much the dog howls, the moon keeps shining (Luke 9:51). Big people aren't intimidated by small people.

☆

998. If you avoid evil, it's a good chance that evil will avoid you (Prov. 8:13; 1 Thes. 5:22).

☆

999. The best time to plant a tree is today (Eccl. 3:1-11).

☆

1000. What's impossible today might be possible tomorrow (Matt. 19:26).

☆

1001. Rejection is nothing but God's direction (Acts 13:46-48).

☆

1002. Good seeds won't grow to their fullest potential in bad soil (Luke 8:5-8). Atmosphere and environment are very important.

☆

1003. If your thinking is limited, then your life will be limited (Rom. 12:2).

☆

1004. Whatever you do in life, give it your all or don't do it at all (Eccl. 9:10).

☆

1005. Spend less than you make and invest the rest (Prov. 6:6-8). Work for your money and then let your money work for you.

☆

1006. Nobody resents kind words (Prov. 15:1).

☆

1007. Death puts life in its proper perspective (Eccl. 7:1-2).

☆

1008. God's plan will often span more than one generation (Exd. 33:1). Think generational.

☆

1009. Learn to ponder principles, frame facts and treasurer truths (Luke 2:19; 51).

☆

1010. Don't let your anger get the best of you (Eph. 4:26).

☆

1011. Don't just live your life, lead your life by making good choices (Prov. 3:5-6).

☆

1012. If you don't cure it, you will have to learn to endure it (Num. 33:55).

☆

1013. Don't let your problems overshadow your possibilities (Luke 1:37).

☆

1014. Movement creates friction. If you are trying to make progress, expect opposition (Eph. 6:10-17).

☆

1015. When you announce your dream, it will expose your friends and your foes (Gen. 37:5-11).

☆

1016. The law of attractions says, you attract who you are not who you want (Prov. 13:20).

☆

1017. God is a God who opens doors (Rev. 3:8). When He does, answer the door because opportunity waits for no one.

☆

1018. Behind all achievement is a strong desire. (Napolen Hill)

☆

1019. Necessity is the mother of all inventions. (Benjamin Franklin)

☆

1020. A stagnant mind is the breeding ground for fear (2 Tim. 1:7).

☆

1021. Self-control is the result of thought control (2 Cor. 10:4-5).

☆

1022. Proper rest increases your productivity and creativity (Mark 1:35). You can't be productive without a lot of energy.

☆

1023. Strength grows out of resistance and struggle (1 Pet. 5:10).

☆

1024. Habits are first cobwebs, then cables. (Spanish Proverb)

☆

1025. Giving destroys the demons of greed and selfishness (Luke 12:15-21; Acts 20:35).

☆

1026. Bad habits are like comfortable beds--easy to get into but hard to get out of. (Waston C. Black)

☆

1027. The door to success is always marked "push" (Phil. 4:13).

☆

1028. Organized knowledge and effort is power. (Napolen Hill)

☆

1029. Knowing how to find knowledge is the first step toward wisdom (James 1:5).

☆

1030. Ideas are capital that bears interests only in the hands of talent. (Antoine Rivaroli)

☆

1031. Those who do not read must depend on those who do (Dan. 5:1-31).

1032. Document your discoveries so you won't have to rediscover them later (Rev. 1:19). Use a daily journal to help you.

1033. Right thinking is mental success. Right action leads to material success (Josh. 1:8; Ps. 1:1-3).

1034. An invasion of armies can be resisted, but not an idea whose time has come. (Victor Hugo)

1035. Creation is proof that there is a Creator (Gen. 1:1; Heb. 3:4).

1036. If you read broadly you can be used widely (Acts 17:16-32; Phil. 3:4-6).

1037. To get the BEST out of people. Believe in them. Encourage them. Support them. Trust them. (John C. Maxwell)

1038. Greatness requires focus. Focus is the ability to say "No" to people and things you shouldn't do (Phil. 3:13; Heb. 12:2).

1039. Help your brother's boat across and lo! You own has reached the shore. (Hindu Proverb)

1040. Action separates winners from losers more than anything else in life. (Jack Canfield)

1041. Principles are laws that cannot be broken (John 10:35). If you break them they will break you (Matt. 21:42-46).

☆

1042. God is the first cause that was uncaused (Rev. 22:13).

☆

1043. An atheist is one who has great faith in nothing (Ps. 14:1; 55:1). That's why the Bible calls him a fool.

☆

1044. A spirit of fear will keep you from achieving and enjoying much in life (2 Tim. 1:7).

☆

1045. Grateful people are loyal people (John 19:26-27).

☆

1046. Success is usually on the other side of defeat or adversity (Job 42:10).

☆

1047. Prevention is always better than recovery (Ps. 119:11).

☆

1048. Every person sees through different eyes (2 Kings 6:17).

☆

1049. The clearer your goals, the greater your motivation (Phil. 3:14).

☆

1050. The bigger your dream, the greater your faith (Gen. 12:1-3).

☆

1051. In life, knowing when to say "Yes" and "No" will determine how far you go (Gen. 39:6-10).

☆

1052. Those who constantly rebel will ultimately end up in hell (Rev. 21:8).

☆

1053. Love is the pathway to a person's heart (1 Cor. 13:4-8).

☆

1054. Your confidence will increase with knowledge and experience (Gen. 21:20; 1 Sam. 3:19).

☆

1055. Time management is life management (Ps. 90:12).

☆

1056. A little knowledge can be dangerous if the wrong person has it (Eccl. 9:18).

☆

1057. Thinkers ask questions and followers listen to answers (1 Kings 10:1-5).

☆

1058. The person who doesn't read isn't much different from the person who can't read. (Barbara A. Kipfer)

☆

1059. You can only master that which you do daily (Ps. 119:164).

☆

1060. Your emotions are like elevators, they go up and down (1 Kings 19:1-12). Live your life based upon what you believe.

☆

1061. Put your mind in gear before you put your mouth in motion (Matt. 16:22-23).

☆

1062. Think twice before you speak once (James 1:19-20).

☆

1063. If it's worth having, then it's worth the work and the wait (Gen. 29:18-20).

☆

1064. First a student then a teacher (Matt. 28:19; 2 Tim. 2:2).

☆

1065. Success consists of a series of little daily victories. (Laddie F. Hutar)

☆

1066. Everything must be taught and taught because no one gets it the first time (Is. 28:10).

☆

1067. Teach to impact people not to impress people (Matt. 7:28-29).

☆

1068. There are two parts to learning: thinking and doing (Matt. 21:28-31a).

☆

1069. You have to love people if you want to lead people (John 21:15-17).

☆

1070. Bad leaders are like travel agents. They will send you on a trip alone (Gen. 32:1-21).

☆

1071. Good leaders are like travel guides. They will take the trip with you (Judges 4:8-10; Luke 7:1-6).

☆

1072. Good leaders enlarge people (1 Sam. 16:23). Bad leaders belittle people (1 Sam. 19:9-10).

☆

1073. Losers hate winners because winners remove their excuses for failure (Matt. 27:18).

☆

1074. Focus your time and attention on things you can do something about (John 21:20-22).

☆

1075. God is more anxious to bestow his blessings on us than we are to receive them. (St. Augustine of Hippo)

☆

1076. Character is moral strength (Acts 17:11-12).

☆

1077. We first make our habits then our habits make us (Luke 4:16; Heb. 10:25).

☆

1078. If you are ready, you can answer the door when opportunity knocks (Esther 4:14).

☆

1079. Make-up your mind ahead of time (Dan. 1:8).

☆

1080. In life, there is no such thing as a free lunch (2 Thes. 3:10).

☆

1081. You can do anything you want to do or have to do in life (Phil. 4:13).

☆

1082. Instead of looking for greener pastures, water your own grass (Prov. 5:15-19).

☆

1083. When you decide what you really want, you will figure out a way to get it (Matt. 9:20-22).

☆

1084. Organize for efficiency but prioritize for effectiveness (Neh. 3:1-32).

☆

1085. Being gay is not the way even though society says it's okay (Lev. 18:22; Prov. 14:12; Rom. 1:24-27).

☆

1086. The harder you work the luckier you will get (Deut. 8:18).

☆

1087. Having an abortion is not about a choice but a child (Jer. 1:5; Ps. 139:14-16; Luke 1:25-45).

☆

1088. Success is progressive. Build on the previous day's success (Prov. 4:18).

☆

1089. To move the world we must first move ourselves. (Socrates)

☆

1090. The less you say the more people will remember (Prov. 10:19).

☆

1091. Be where you are mentally, physically and emotionally (Phil. 4:8). Stay focus and enjoy the moment.

☆

1092. Simple words can create great thoughts (Ps. 78:1-6).

☆

1093. To do something big and great, you must let others participate (Eccl. 4:9-12).

☆

1094. Wrong beliefs can cause you much grief (Luke 16:19-31).

☆

1095. The only people who never make any mistakes are in the graveyard (Eccl. 9:10b; Rom. 3:23).

☆

1096. God uses imperfect people because those are the only kind He can find (Rom. 3:23; Ps. 51:5).

☆

1097. The same bucket that can bring water can carry water. Those who talk to you about others will talk to others about you (Prov. 11:13; 16:28; 18:8; 20:19; 26:20; 26:22).

☆

1098. Don't tell everything during your testimony (Rev. 12:11).

☆

1099. Laughter is good medicine for the soul (Prov. 17:22).

☆

1100. If more people would get in the health line, we would have less people in the healing line (Prov. 3:7-8).

☆

1101. Always consider the source before you take advice from others. If their advice isn't working for them, it probably won't work for you (Prov. 11:14).

☆

1102. Character is the sum total of all our everyday choices. (Margaret Jensen)

☆

1103. It's not how long you live that counts, but how well you live (Gen. 15:15).

☆

1104. Faith is the ability to see God in the dark (2 Cor. 5:7).

☆

1105. The road to greatness begins at home. (Chinese Proverb)

☆

1106. If you hit rock bottom, remember that Jesus is the Rock in the bottom (1 Cor. 10:4).

☆

1107. As a man thinks so is he, and as a man continues to think so will he be (Prov. 23:7a).

☆

1108. You can lead a horse to the water but you can't make him drink. Likewise, you can lead a fool to a book but you can't make him think (2 Tim. 3:6-7).

☆

1109. HALT before you make a decision. Never make a decision when you're **H**urting, **A**ngry, **L**onely or **T**ired. (Rev. Kevin Bryant)

☆

1110. Give me a fish and I eat for a day. Teach me to fish and I eat for life. (Chinese Proverb)

☆

1111. If you don't obey God, He may send you to Whale University (Jonah 1:17). Eventually you'll learn the lesson.

☆

1112. The only alternative to growth is death. Don't die from the neck up while you are still alive (1 Tim. 5:6).

☆

1113. People like what people like whether it's wrong or right (1 Sam. 8:4-22).

☆

1114. God will give you everything you need in to order to make it regardless of the economy (Gen. 26:1-14; Ps. 37:25).

☆

1115. You can't choose your family members, but you can pick you friends (Prov. 18:24). Your friends are a reflection of you.

☆

1116. Get all the education you can because that's the one thing no one can take away from you. (John T. Lewis)

☆

1117. Learn as many skills as you can because you don't know which skill you'll have to use to earn a living. (John T. Lewis)

☆

1118. Take your children to church with you. If you don't raise them right, some day you'll live to regret it. (John T. Lewis)

☆

1119. God came to Adam and Eve in the cool of the day. Don't deal with people when you're angry. (John T. Lewis)

☆

1120. When you mess up, admit it and ask for forgiveness. People will forgive you if you admit you made a mistake. (John T. Lewis)

☆

In Loving Memory of the late John T. Lewis
October 19, 1921 -- December 19, 2003

Pearls of Wisdom for Everyday Living Journal by Rev. Amos L. Lewis provides 365 days of wisdom and can be used in conjunction with this book to help you in your own, daily devotionals.

Use Rev. Lewis' *Pearls of Wisdom for Everyday Living Journal* to record your own Pearls of Wisdom! To order your journal or more copies of this book for your family and friends, please visit *www.onechoicecanchangealife.com,* contact A.L.Lewis Ministries at *www.allewisministries.org* or write to Amethyst Moon Publishing, P.O. Box 87885, Tucson, AZ 85754.

TO YOUR SUCCESS

Success is living in such a way that you are using what God has given you--your intellect, abilities, and energy--to reach the purpose that he intends for your life. (Kathi Hudson)

The most important single ingredient in the formula of success is knowing how to get along with people. (Theodore Roosevelt)

There is a four-word formula for success that applies equally well to organizations and individuals--*make yourself more useful.*
(Author Unknown)

There are no victories at bargain prices. (Dwight D. Eisenhower)

The success of a great person is doing what others will not do.
(Author Unknown)

Success in life is a matter not so much of talent as of concentration and perseverance. (C. W. Wendle)

Most people who succeed in the face of seemingly impossible conditions are people who simply don't know how to quit.
(Robert H. Schuller)

Success is measured not so much by the position that one has reached in life as by the obstacles he has overcome while trying to succeed.
(Booker T. Washington)

Success is for the those energetic enough to work for it, hopeful enough to look for it, patient enough to wait for it, brave enough to seize it, and strong enough to hold it. (Author Unknown)

Success equals effort plus vision. (Author Unknown)

Success is not a matter of pure luck. It is mainly a matter of first, work; second, work; third, work--with, of course, a plentiful mixture of brains, foresight, and imagination. (B. C. Forbes)

Striving for success without hard work is like trying to harvest where you haven't planted. (David Bly)

The Lord gave us two ends--one to sit on and the other to think on. Success depends on which one we use the most. (Ann Landers)

A successful person is one who went ahead and did the thing the rest of us never quite got around to. (Author Unknown)

There is not success without honor; no happiness without a clear conscience; no use in living at all if only for one's self.
(Robert Waters)

The man who gets ahead is the one who does more than is necessary and keeps on doing it. (Author Unknown)

Success is getting what you want; happiness is wanting what you get. (Mike Murdock)

If there is any one secret of success, it lies in the ability to get the other person's point of view and see things from his angle as well as your own. (Henry Ford)

Many successful people today were failures yesterday, who never gave up. (Author Unknown)

Science says that success is relative. Once you become successful then come all the relatives. (Author Unknown)

The road to success is marked with many tempting parking spaces. (Author Unknown)

The price of success is perseverance. The price of failure comes cheaper. (Author Unknown)

It takes the hammer of persistence to drive the nail of success (John Mason)

Failure, rejection, and mistakes are the perfect stepping stones to success. (Alan Goldberg)

Plan for the day. Since you don't know on which day success will occur, you'd better be ready every day. (Jeffrey Gitomer)

The only place where success comes before work is in the dictionary. (Author Unknown)

BONUS SECTION

If Jesus were born one thousand times in Bethlehem and not in me, then I would still be lost. (Corrie ten Boom)

The repetition of small efforts will accomplish more than the occasional use of great talents. (Charles H. Spurgeon)

Some people are like blisters. They don't show up until the work is done. (Author Unknown)

Life's most urgent question is: What are you doing for others? (Dr. Martin Luther King, Jr.)

In this world it is not what we take up, but what we give up, that makes us rich. (Henry Ward Beecher)

Only a life lived for others is worth living. (Albert Einstein)

You aren't wealthy until you have something money can't buy. (Garth Brooks)

When the character of a man is not clear to you, look at his friends. (Japanese Proverb)

You only believe the part of the Bible you do. (Rick Warren)

Pray, and let God worry. (Martin Luther)

Make no small plans. For they have no power to stir humanity's blood. (Daniel Burnham)

The highest reward for a person's work is not what they get for it, but what they become because of it. (John Ruskin)

Guard well your spare moments. They are like uncut diamonds. Discard them and their value will never be known. Improve them and they will become the brightest gems in a useful life.
(Ralph Waldo Emerson)

Things which matter most must never be at the mercy of things that matter least. (Johann Wolfgang von Goethe)

Your vision has not truly captured your heart until it captures your wallet. (Andy Stanley)

Concerning all acts of initiative and creation, there is one elementary truth--that the moment one definitely commits oneself, then Providence moves, too. (Johann Wolfgang von Goethe)

You can't stop the waves, but you can learn to surf. (Jonkbat-Zinn)

If you make a sale, you earn a commission. If you make a friend, you can earn a fortune. (Jeffrey Gitomer)

Some people regard discipline as a chore. For me, it is a kind of order that sets me free to fly. (Julie Andrews)

I look forward to being older, when what you look like becomes less and less the issue, and what you are is the point. (Susan Sarandon)

Handle them carefully, for words have more power than atom bombs. (Pearl Strachan)

People do not lack strength; they lack will. (Victor Hugo)

Discouragement comes when you try to start with what you wish you had but don't have. And it intensifies when you insist on trying to be in a position you are not in and probably never will be in. (Stuart Briscoe)

Between the great things we can't do and the little things we won't do, the danger is we shall do nothing. (Author Unknown)

Luck is what happens when preparation meets opportunity. (Author Unknown)

It's time for us to turn to each other, not on each other. (Jesse L. Jackson)

In a boxing match you can lose the first 14 rounds. But all you have to do is nail your opponent in the last ten seconds of the 15th round and you're the heavyweight champion. (Ross Perot)

Failure should be our teacher, not our undertaker. Failure is delay not defeat. It is a temporary detour, not a dead-end street. (Author Unknown)

In the game of life it's a good idea to have a few early losses, which relieves you of the pressure of trying to maintain an undefeated season. (Bill Baughan)

A man is not defeated by his opponents but by himself. (Jan Christian Smuts)

We must view young people not as empty bottles to be filled, but as candles to be lit. (Robert H. Shaffer)

Criticism, like rain, should be gentle enough to nourish one's growth without destroying one's roots. (Author Unknown)

Be more concerned with your character than with your reputation. Your character is what you really are while your reputation is merely what others think you are. (Dale Carnegie)

Courage is resistance to fear, mastery of fear, not absence of fear. (Mark Twain)

The real art of conversation is not only to say the right thing in the right place, but to leave unsaid the wrong thing at the tempting moment. (Dorothy Nevell)

A Winner's Creed by Ralph Waldo Emerson

If you think you are beaten, you are; if you think you dare not, you don't. If you'd like to win, but think you can't, it's almost a cinch you won't. If you think you'll lose, you're lost, for out in the world we find success begins with a person's faith; it's all in the state of mind. Life's battles don't always go to the stronger or the faster hand; they go to the one who trusts in God and always thinks, "I can."

Love is a fruit in season at all times, and within reach of every hand. (Mother Teresa)

Love lights more fire than hate extinguishes. (Ella Wheller Wilcox)

Goal setting and goal achievement is a science and self-discipline that must be practiced every day. (Jeffrey Gitomer)

Death is not the end for someone who has faith.
(Archbishop Desmond Tutu)

If it weren't for the dark days, we wouldn't know what it is to walk in the light. (Earl Campbell)

A man is not hurt so much by what happens, as by his opinion of what happens. (Michel de Montaigne)

Every thought is a seed. If you plant crab apples, don't count on harvesting Golden Delicious. (Bill Meyer)

Attitude --You were born to win—but you must plan to win, prepare to win, then you can expect to win. (Jeffrey Gitomer)

Don't think there are no crocodiles because the water is calm. (Malayan Proverb)

2/3 of PROMOTION is MOTION. (Author Unknown)

Actions are the only way to bridge plans and goals with accomplishment. Nothing happens until you do something to make it happen—every day. (Jeffrey Gitomer)

The young do not know enough to be prudent, and therefore they attempt the impossible, and achieve it, generation after generation. (Pearl S. Buck)

In order for you to profit from your mistakes, you have to get out and make some. (Anonymous)

Kind words can be short and easy to speak, but their echoes are truly endless. (Mother Teresa)

Become valuable. The more valuable you become, the more the marketplace will reward you. Become known as a resource, not a salesperson. Your value is linked to your knowledge and your willingness to help others. (Jeffrey Gitomer)

If you want to be happy, set a goal that commands your thoughts, liberates your energy, and inspires your hopes. (Andrew Carnegie)

Expose yourself to what's new. If you're not learning every day-- your competition is. (Jeffrey Gitomer)

A candle loses nothing by lighting another candle.
(Father James Keller)

A life isn't important except for the impact it has on others.
(Words from Jackie Robinson's Tomb Stone)

Beware of little expenses; a small leak will sink a great ship. (Benjamin Franklin)

Our days are like scrolls: write on them what you want to be remembered for. (Bahya Ibn Paquda)

A goal is a dream with an ending. (Duke Ellington)

The future belongs to those who believe in the beauty of their dreams. (Eleanor Roosevelt)

When your heart speaks, take good notes. (Judith Campbell)

Faith is an oasis in the heart which can never be reached by the caravan of thinking. (Kahlil Gibran)

It is only with the heart that one can see rightly; what is essential is invisible to the eye. (Antoine de Saint-Exupry)

To those who can dream there is no such place as far away. (Anonymous)

Your vision will become clear only when you look into your heart. Who looks outside, dreams. Who looks inside, awakens. (Carl Jung)

The distance a person goes is not as important as the direction. (Author Unknown)

Leaders share responsibility. They don't dictate, they set examples for others to follow. (Jeffrey Gitomer)

Sometimes it takes a painful experience to make us change our ways (Proverbs 20:30). (Good News Bible in Today's English Version)

The biggest risk is to never take one. Leaders are determined to win or try again. (Jeffrey Gitomer)

The greatest discovery of my generation is that human beings can alter their lives by changing their attitude of mind. (William James)

If you have much, give of your wealth; if you have little, give of your heart. (Author Unknown)

If you're having a hard time following, you might try leading. (Jeffrey Gitomer)

A man that controls his mind controls his future. (Author Unknown)

If you have knowledge, let others light their candles with it.
(Winston Churchill)

It is a funny thing about life. If you refuse to accept anything but the best, you very often get it. (W. Somerset Maugham)

We are what we repeatedly do. Excellence is therefore not an act, but a habit. (Aristotle)

Freedom bestows on us the priceless gift of opportunity—if we neglect our opportunities we shall certainly lose our freedom. (Dwight D. Eisenhower)

When Christians work together, they divide the effort and multiply the effect. (July 2, 1999, Our Daily Bread)

Life is either a daring adventure or nothing. (Helen Keller)

Nothing is really works unless you would rather be doing something else. (J. M. Barrie)

Wisdom consists in knowing what to do with what you know.
(Bits and Pieces)

If we take care of our character, our reputation will take care of itself! (D. L. Moody)

Always do right. This will gratify some people and astonish the rest.
(Mark Twain)

Never undertake anything for which you would not have the courage to ask the blessing of Heaven. (George Christopher Lichtenberg)

The art of being wise is the art of knowing what to overlook.
(William James)

Never attempt to bear more than one kind of trouble at once. Some people bear three kinds--all they have had, all they have now, and all they expect to have. (Edward Everett Hale)

A truth that's told with bad intent beats all the lies you can invent. (William Blake)

Every man has a right to be wrong in his opinions. But no man has a right to be wrong in his facts. (Bernard Baruch)

It is only with the heart that one can see rightly. What is essential is invisible to the eye. (The Little Prince)

A champion is one who gets up even when he can't.
(Jack Dempsey)

I can do only one thing at a time, but I can avoid doing many things simultaneously. (Asleigh Brilliant)

Before a brilliant person begins something great, he must look foolish to the crowd. (I Ching)

You can fool some of the people all of the time, and all of the people some of the time; but you can't fool all of the people all of the time. (Abraham Lincoln)

When you say a situation or a person is hopeless, you are slamming the door in the face of God. (Reverend Charles Allen)

If God were not willing to forgive sin, heaven would be empty. (German Proverb)

If you wish to know the road ahead, inquire of those who have traveled it. (Chinese Proverb)

How do you go about setting a goal and achieving it? There are three steps:
1. To get what you want, you must first know what you want.
2. You must believe you will get it with your whole heart and mind.
3. Finally, you must work toward the goal with regularity.
(Author Unknown)

A wise, mature person is known for his understanding. The more pleasant his words, the more persuasive he is (Proverbs 16:21). (TEV)

Intelligent people think before they speak; what they say is then more persuasive (Proverbs 16:23). (TEV)

He is no fool who gives what he cannot keep to gain what he cannot lose. (Jim Elliot)

Many great ideas have been lost because the people who had them could not stand being laughed at. (Author Unknown)

Intelligent people are always eager and ready to learn. (Proverbs 18:15). (TEV)

Service is the rent you pay for room on this earth. (Shirley Chisholm)

If you want people to like you, forgive them when they wrong you. Remembering wrongs can break up a friendship (Proverbs 17:9).

Being cheerful keeps you healthy. It is slow death to be gloomy all the time (Proverbs 17:22). (TEV)

Marriages may be made in heaven, but man is responsible for the maintenance work. (Changing Times)

Do yourself a favor and learn all you can; then remember what you learn and you will prosper (Proverbs 19:8). (TEV)

If you listen to advice and are willing to learn, one day you will be wise (Proverbs 19:20). (TEV)

My child, when you stop learning, you will soon neglect what you already know (Proverbs 19:27). (TEV)

The oil of courtesy takes the friction out of life. (NBC USA, Inc., Web Page)

I hope I shall always possess firmness and virtue enough to maintain (what I consider the most enviable of all titles) the character of an honest man. (George Washington)

Wise people live in wealth and luxury, but stupid people spend their money as fast as they get it (Proverbs 21:20). (TEV)

When spider webs unite, they can tie up a lion. (Ethiopian Proverb)

Never let yourself think that you are wiser than you are; simply obey the Lord and refuse to do wrong (Proverbs 3:7). (TEV)

But what is freedom? Rightly understood, A universal license to be good. (Hartley Coleridge)

Troubles are like babies—they only grow if you nurse them. (Author Unknown)

Always remember what you have learned. Your education is your life, guard it well (Proverbs 13:4). (TEV)

Be careful how you think; your life is shaped by your thoughts (Proverbs 13:23). (TEV)

Plan carefully what you do, and whatever you do will turn out right (Proverbs 13:26). (TEV)

If you tell the truth you don't have to remember anything. (Mark Twain)

If you correct conceited people, you will only be insulted. If you reprimand evil people, you will only get hurt (Proverbs 9:7). (TEV)

Never correct conceited people; they will hate you for it. But if you correct the wise, they will respect you (Proverbs 9:8). (TEV)

Anything you say to the wise will make them wiser. Whatever you tell the righteous will add to their knowledge (Proverbs 9:9). (TEV)

If we take on the challenge of continually developing ourselves, building ourselves, learning and growing, becoming more knowledgeable, stronger, improving our vocabulary and our skills and our education and training, there is no height that we cannot reach. (Brian Tracy)

What a man needs to get ahead is a powerful enemy. (Wendle Wilkie)

Our antagonist is our helper. He that wrestles with us strengthens our muscles and sharpens our skill. (Edmund Burke)

Knowledge, properly applied, is power. (Earl Nightingale)

Our ability to translate our thoughts and ideas into words, in a powerful and effective way, is inextricably linked to our growth in the world of business, or any other organization. (Earl Nightingale)

Learning gives us more life, freedom and happiness. (Zig Ziglar)

People with rich vocabularies have a multihued palette of colors with which to paint their experience, not only for others, but for themselves as well. (Anthony Robbins)

Mistakes are your stepping stones. They are your teachers. Don't punish yourself for making a mistake. If you are willing to learn and grow from the mistake, then it serves as a step toward fulfillment in your life. (Louise L. Hay)

Man's extremity is God's opportunity. (J. B. Phillips)

Be generous, and you will be prosperous. Help others, and you will be helped (Proverbs 11:25) (TEV).

The best way to meet trouble is to face it. (Author Unknown)

The reason why worry kills more people than work is that more people worry than work. (Robert Frost)

A real friend is one who, when you've made a fool of yourself, lets you forget it. (Author Unknown)

The key to happiness in life is learning to focus on the donut instead of the hole. (Author Unknown)

Insanity is doing the same thing over and over while expecting a different result. (Author Unknown)

The three grand essentials of happiness are: something to do, someone to love, and something to hope for. (Alexander Chalmers)

A sense of humor is the pole that adds balance to our steps as we walk the tightrope of life. (Author Unknown)

Wise people live in wealth and luxury, but stupid people spend their money as fast as they get it (Proverbs 21:20). (TEV)

Goals are the road map to success. Everyone knows that, but less than 5% of our society sets and achieves them. (Author Unknown)

Is God impressed with gifts you bring?
Your work, your skills, each little thing?
Oh yes, He values what you do,
But what He wants is time with you. (Gustafson)

I use not only all the brains I have, but all I can borrow.
(Woodrow Wilson)

A fool and his money are soon parted. (Benjamin Franklin)

Our life is what our thoughts make it. (Marcus Aurelius)

The only way to live happily with people is to overlook their faults and admire their virtues. (Author Unknown)

Intelligence and character have always been the goal of real education. (Dr. Martin Luther King, Jr.)

The more you read, the more you know. The more you know, the smarter you grow. The smarter you grow, the stronger your voice; when speaking your mind or making your choice.
(Author Unknown)

The tragedy of life doesn't lie in not reaching your goal. The tragedy lies in having no goal to reach. (Benjamin E. Mays)

If there is no struggle, there is no progress. (Frederick Douglas)

Money doesn't make the man. Some people have money, and some people are rich. (Thomas A. Dorsey)

Don't face the day until you've faced God. (Maya Angelou)

The first and best victory is to conquer self. (Plato)

There is in this world no such force as the force of a man determined to rise. The human soul cannot be permanently chained.
(W. E. B. Dubois)

Learn to see, listen, and think for yourself. (Malcom X)

There are no shade trees on the road to success.
(Bishop Leontine Kelly)

Hunter in pursuit of an elephant does not stop to throw stones at birds. (Uganda Proverb)

For wisdom is more precious than rubies, and nothing you desire can compare with her (Proverbs 8:11, NIV).

How much better to get wisdom than gold, to choose understanding rather than silver (Proverbs 16:16, NIV)!

All the earth sought to Solomon, to hear his Wisdom, which God had put in his heart (1 Kings 10:24, KJV).

Trophies are given out after you cross the finish line. (Bill Purvis)

IN CLOSING.....

If this book has proven to be a blessing to you, you can find additional resources by visiting the website at *www.allewisministries.org*

I want to thank you from the bottom of my heart for being a part of this ministry by purchasing a copy of this book. I hope these pearls of wisdom will continue to inspire you as you fulfill your God-given destiny in life. Remember this powerful truth: "If you don't put a limit on God, He won't put any limits on you."

If you would like to know God through a personal relationship with Jesus Christ (John 3:16 and John 17:3), then follow the Romans' Road presented on the next page.

Life is short.
Death is sure.
Sin is the problem.
Christ is the cure.
(Author Unknown)

ROMANS' ROAD TO SALVATION

Romans 3:10
As it is written, there is **none righteous**, no not one.

Romans 3:23
For **all have sinned**, and come short of the glory of God.

Romans 6:23
For the **wages of sin is death**; but the gift of God is eternal life through Jesus Christ our Lord.

Romans 5:8
But **God commendeth His love toward us**, in that, while we were yet sinners, Christ died for us.

Romans 10:9-10
That if thou shalt **confess** with thy mouth, the Lord Jesus, and shalt **believe** in thine heart that God hath raised Him from the dead, thou shalt be saved. For with the heart man believes unto righteousness; and with the mouth confession is made unto **salvation**.

Romans 10:13
For **whosoever shall call** upon the name of the Lord shall be saved.

Lord Jesus, I realize that I am a sinner. I believe you died for my sins. Please forgive me of my sins. Come into my heart and be my personal savior. Thank you for saving me and giving me eternal life. In Jesus' Name, I pray, Amen.

∞∞∞

Oh, God Thou has made us for Thyself, and our hearts find no rest until they rest in Thee. (Augustine)

BIOGRAPHY OF PASTOR AMOS L. LEWIS

Pastor Amos L. Lewis is the son of Sarah Lewis and the late John T. Lewis of Pinckard, Alabama. He graduated from Dale County High School and became the first African-American to win the prestigious John Philip Sousa Band Award. After High School, he joined the United States Air Force where he continued his education earning both an Associates of Liberal Arts Degree from St. Leo College and a Bachelor of Science Degree in Church Ministries from Liberty University. After 21 years of honorable service, Pastor Lewis retired as a Master Sergeant and became the full-time Senior Pastor of Rising Star Missionary Baptist Church.

Pastor Lewis was licensed to preach in June 1983 at St. Paul Missionary Baptist Church in Pinckard, Alabama. While servicing in the Air Force, he stayed busy serving the Lord as an Associate Minister at the Glendale Baptist Church in Miami, Florida. It was at this church that he met and married his lovely wife, Zeannie Lewis. Pastor Lewis served as a Church Training Union Teacher for teenagers, a Royal Ambassadors Counselor for little boys, a Trumpet Player in the Music Department, and as a Bible Study Teacher at a local Correctional Facility.

After being reassigned to Davis-Monthan AFB in June 1984, Pastor Lewis and Sis. Lewis joined First Southern Baptist Church under the leadership of Pastor Ron Hart. They served faithfully in the Bus Ministry and Sunday School Department for about a year. The Lord then led them to joined Trinity Missionary Baptist Church where he served as an Associate Minister. Recognizing his heart for ministry, Pastor Earnest L. Girley ordained Pastor Lewis in September 1986. Shortly thereafter, he was called to serve as Assistant Pastor of

Rising Star Missionary Baptist Church from January 1987 until he was officially called as Pastor in May 1987. He was installed as Pastor of Rising Star by Pastor Girley in June 1987.

Through his anointed and innovative leadership, Pastor Lewis continues to lead the church to new levels in ministry for kingdom building. Rising Star is fast becoming a model church for ministry in the community. Because of his passion for the Body of Christ and Community, he serves as the Moderator of the Southern Arizona Missionary Baptist District Association, former President of the Paradise Baptist State Convention Minister's Conference, and former President of the Interdenominational Ministerial Alliance (IMA) of Tucson and Vicinity.

In March 2007, Pastor Lewis led Rising Star to locate to their 4.3 acres campus where they built a 2.5 million dollars start-of-the-art multipurpose facility. Currently, the church has a membership over 850 people and over 50 ministries.

Because of Pastor Lewis' passion for growth and service, he continues to pursue higher learning. He has a Master's Degree in Leadership Development from Koinonia Christian College. Pastor Lewis is a mentor to many ministers and leaders.

Pastor Lewis is married to Zeannie Lewis and they are the proud parents of four lovely children: Kelvin (his wife Tracey and their son Jayden), Jenelle, Jeremiah and Terria (her son Emmanuel Z. Holmes).

Pearls of Wisdom Notes